FAMILY CAMPING

MONTIE ROLAND

CONTENTS

PROLOGUE 5
ONE: WHY CAMP 9
TWO: TYPES OF CAMPING 17
THREE: FINDING PRICELESS MOMENTS 29
FOUR: IMPORTANCE OF TRADITIONS 33
FIVE: WHAT TO DO WHEN YOU ARE CAMPING 43
SIX: TYPES OF TENTS 57
SEVEN: FORGET SLEEPING BAGS, THINK SLEEP SYSTEM ... 65
EIGHT: CLOTHING FOR CAMPING 79
NINE: BUILDING A CAMPFIRE 91
TEN: HOW TO DRESS IN LAYERS 103
ELEVEN: BREAKFAST - DO'S AND DON'TS 117
TWELVE: CAMPING - LUNCH 127
THIRTEEN: CAMPING - DINNER 133
FOURTEEN: CAMPFIRE JOYS 145
FIFTEEN: WEATHER AND CAMPING 155
SIXTEEN: BREAKING CAMP 165
SNEAK PEEK: HIKING 177

FAMILY CAMPING

Copyright © 2019, Montie Roland

All rights reserved. Reproduction in part or in whole is strictly forbidden without the express written consent of the publisher.

Cover and interior design by Roseanna White Designs
Cover illustrations from Shutterstock

ISBNS: 978-1-7335969-2-3 (print)
            978-1-7335969-1-6 (digital)

PROLOGUE

The word "camping" inspires smiles in many people. My goal is to show you how to create memorable family experiences in the woods. First off, I'd like to thank you for buying this book. If you're about to embark on your first camping trip then forge ahead and let me share what I've learned over the years. On the other hand, if you've camped a few times and are looking for tips on how to be more efficient and accomplished in your future trips, then read on. I always say *knowledge weighs nothing*. My hope is that you'll find yourself better informed after reading this book.

Allow me to share a little about myself. As a graduate of North Carolina State University, my day job is mechanical engineering specializing in new product development. I was raised in Asheville, NC, where I earned my Eagle Scout award. Growing up, our home was located only a few miles from the Blue Ridge Parkway, so I had many blessed opportunities to spend time outside. My childhood was an exceptional gateway to outdoor adventure for an inquisitive kid with tons of time and a vivid imagination.

As an avid outdoor enthusiast, I'd say my happy place is being in the woods. Over the years, I've had the opportunity to camp in North Carolina, Virginia, and New Mexico. The trip to New Mexico was a ninety mile backpacking trip to Philmont, the famous Boy Scout reservation. These rich experiences have molded me into the man I am today.

My wife and I own land in the mountains near Hot Springs, NC, where we hope to build a cabin sometime over the next couple of years. Until then, Connie and I enjoy tent camping there several times a year.

Amazing hiking on Grandfather Mountain

During the final edit of this book, we camped near Blowing Rock, NC, and hiked the Profile Trail up Grandfather Mountain. What a glorious hike and memorable weekend enjoying tent camping just off the Blue Ridge Parkway.

I have found that camping is a great way to enjoy nature while keeping your trips inexpensive. When you camp, you save money so you can spread your funds over more excursions and spend more time outdoors—which is a win-win for everybody involved! Just like everyone else who works nine-to-five, I struggle with my work life balance. Throw in family and responsibilities at home, you quickly realize you must carve out time to do what you enjoy.

This book covers a lot of skills and topics that apply to camping in your area and at different stages of life. Camping is a great experience for your family. Hopefully *Family Camping* (Montie's Guide to Camping, Book One) helps you escape your daily life and enjoy the outdoors!

Linville Gorge

ONE

WHY CAMP

So, you've almost decided to go camping; but you're wondering what you can expect. Will there be stress or relaxation? You may experience physical pain from usually unused muscles, or perhaps the benefits will outweigh the perceived negatives. This is a good thought process to have. In my mind, the physical and mental benefits of camping will push you over the edge and you'll start planning your trip before you hit the second chapter.

PROPERLY PLANNED CAMPING TRIPS CAN CAUSE RELAXATION

Planned properly, camping can be relaxing. But, beware of the potential physical exhaustion which can occur with ill-informed choices. Depending on decisions like where you go, how you camp, the length of your stay, and what you bring, relaxation may only be a longed-for dream. But there is hope, so keep on reading and I'll help you design a successful camping trip.

IMPROVE ATTITUDE

Often times, getting out of your current environment and replacing your daily concerns with activities like building a fire, sleeping in a sleeping bag, or making s'mores over a campfire can help to push out your usual concerns and allow you to relax in the comfort of simplicity. You get a fresh perspective on life and family that you wouldn't normally get in the day-to-day grind. The campsite is there waiting for you. You just have to take the hardest step of all and walk out your front door and get in the car to head out for an adventure you won't regret.

Connie, Zena and I

Personally, I feel at home in the mountains. I love being there with the views and the hikes and the trees. The people and music are great. There are so many awesome things to see and do there. Find your passion by going out and experiencing the world. You can experience it slow, in a tent or on foot. You'll see views from your campsite and on your hikes that you'll totally miss through your car window or on your TV. Just go and enjoy the journey.

A NEW NORMAL PROVIDES INSTANT GRATIFICATION

When we get away and into a different context, our brain can back-out of the humdrum or stress of day-to-day life. While camping you are in a temporary new routine, which can be a nice health adjustment for your mind. Mentally we push out concerns from the old normal and replace them with immediate activities. This process allows instant gratification by being out of your ordinary circumstance.

EXERCISE BENEFIT

When you camp, you're not performing your normal activities so your body adapts to what you ask of it. We fall into ruts by repetitively doing the same physical exercises. Conversely, there are times we do nothing. While camping, you're throwing new actions at your body and those new endeavors keep you in motion much of the time, they also challenge your body and spirit. That is a good thing. You may be tired at the end of the day, but you've recharged your mind and body in a beneficial way that will positively impact you for days or weeks to come after you get back home.

In daily life, you may attempt to minimize your motion. We tend curtail the number of steps while cooking a meal or travel to our job with the shortest route, or in our office most of us sit around typing on a computer. While camping, we're in a position where we can be constantly moving which forces our bodies to adjust. What that means is that we're burning energy on creative work which I think is very enjoyable and rewarding.

NO INTERRUPTIONS
ALLOW FOR DEEP CONVERSATIONS

Possibly, the most wonderful thing about camping is the one-on-one time spent with loved ones without the normal of interruptions of daily life. When at home or at work, many things demand our attention. But, when camping, it's a totally different situation. Diverse issues vie for our concentration. Cell coverage may be non-existent or limited. Because of this, there's a good chance you're going to have conversations at a level you probably didn't otherwise. At home you can turn on the TV or pick up your phone or login to your computer to check email. When camping, you may not even have a cell signal. Sitting around the campfire with laughter filling the air and joy in your hearts, that's the goal.

You will want to plan ahead for how to handle electronic usage at the campsite. Today's kids are often addicted or borderline addicted to constant contact through a smart phone. If you totally take them away, that may create frustrations that will keep your children from enjoying the trip. It may be that no electronics use is too much to ask, that may seem like punishment. Look beyond the whining and moaning and complaining and figure out a win-win situation that works for your family. Your kids win because they are looking up from their phone long enough to enjoy the outdoors. So if completely taking away the phones is going to really be an impediment to them savoring the weekend, then allow your kids to use them a couple of hours a day. Another option is to not let them recharge electronics. When the battery dies, then your phone usage ends for the weekend. This is a great way to teach them how to budget a resource. Whatever you do, let your children know a set of clear rules. Camping is a new situation for everyone and if letting you kids have their phones for a few minutes makes them more receptive to camping, then maybe that is a good plan.

SEEK OUT PRICELESS MOMENTS

One of the things I crave and look forward to when camping are priceless moments. You may be alone and look out across the valley to see the opposite mountain or you may take in a deep breath and enjoy the rare view. It may just be you because you're the first one up in the morning and you're enjoying the quiet and the beauty. Or perhaps someone you love laughs which makes you revel in joy. Possibly you're the one laughing. Maybe everyone is laughing around the campfire.

Camping is one of the greatest ways to generate these special times. In later chapters we'll talk about the ways you can set yourself up for success or failure. If you let them, you will find priceless moments camping. Then you will have memories and stories that you and your kids will cherish for years to come.

I saw a meme on Pinterest that had a Prius at the top of the image, and at the bottom a Jeep in the desert sitting on the crest of a hill, in front of a sunset. A guy and his kids are in the Jeep enjoying the sun setting in this majestic place. The closing message of the meme said, "Your kids will never, ever remember you getting fifty-five miles per gallon. However, they will remember the night you watched the sun set over the mountains."

BE RECEPTIVE TO WHAT WILL BE BEAUTIFUL MEMORIES

One way to generate your own memories is through camping. My goal in this book is to lead you through how to discover them. When you are well prepared, have knowledge and training and proper equipment, then, you've put some of the adversity behind you and you're in a good situation for those priceless moments to occur.

The all you have to do is be receptive to catch them and revel in them.

Knowledge is power and weighs nothing. You can take this knowledge and couple it with a list of skills for your trip. It is that simple! As you're camping, you're not worried about a sleeping bag getting wet; you're enjoying the memories created with your loved ones.

So, let's get started! I'd be honored if you'd let me share what I've learned and some of my many camping experiences. My hope is this book will enrich your camping trips and help you find those priceless moments.

Great times with the crew

TWO

TYPES OF CAMPING

There are many different levels of engagement when you're camping. Anywhere between an epic adventure like *Man vs. Wild* or perhaps one where more creature comforts are brought from home. Either is fine as long as you can physically pull it off and afford it. The goal is to have a good time and enjoy your time. For me, I like to camp with a tent, I'm not an RV guy. I don't mind taking a shower on the side of the mountain or backpacking in. Sometimes the best way to really see and experience a location is to backpack to the camping site. But, say my wife joins me, she prefers a larger tent, more organization, more creature comforts. If Connie's coming, then what we bring changes and where we stay may change. For both of us to have an enjoyable time, compromises need to happen. Let's talk about some different options.

LIVE OFF THE LAND FOR A WEEKEND

One option would be to head out into the woods with a knife, some tinder, flint and steel, a waterproof jacket, and a wool blanket. The idea is to live off the land for a weekend. If you've got the skills to do it and you enjoy that level of difficulty, go and have fun! There are certainly people that thrive on this primitive I'm-gonna-figure-out-as-I-go-build-me-a-lean-to-in-the-woods-and-feel-close-to-nature type of thing. However, keep in mind your skills and your traveling companions. For example, if you are taking your five-year-old daughter and wife who have never been camping, it would be wise to rethink the details otherwise the trip will end quickly. And, the ride home will be the squirmy kind of uncomfortable.

PURCHASE AN EXPENSIVE RV FOR CAMPING

Another option is to head to your local RV store and buy a half-million dollar motor-home, don't forget your checkbook. Now, you're probably laughing and about to fall off the couch right now as most people don't have that kind of money to invest in a hobby. Or perhaps you have the type of disposable income to make this dream come true. With an RV, you could spend a year driving around the United States. If so, enjoy yourselves and send me a postcard.

But honestly, most of us don't have the means to pay

for a million dollar motor home. So as we look at other forms of camping, be aware of what you can afford. If you want to participate in the RV lifestyle but don't want to buy one, then consider renting one for your trip.

CAMPING SHOULDN'T INVOLVE STRESS OVER MONEY

Because stressing over money doesn't equal fun, keep the scope of your camping trip and equipment in-line with your income. If you have to save for a hundred-dollar tent, instead buy the fifty-dollar option and *choose the contingency* of camping close to home in case a catastrophe happens so you can head home easily. People can enjoy different levels of camping, regardless of their financial ability. Also, consider borrowing supplies from family, friends, or neighbors. Once you decide you want to invest in pieces, you'll know better what works for you.

SURVIVOR MAN VERSUS BACKPACKING

These are two extremes. One is to hike the Appalachian Trail maybe something similar to doing the *Survivor Man* thing for five to seven months. For that epic trip, you'll need to delve into other books to succeed. For this book, let's talk about backpacking. That means you have what you need on your back, and you're going some distance. It may be the whole length of the Appalachian Trail; but more likely it's something like four miles through your local woods.

With backpacking, everyone will bring what they need for the jaunt in their pack. The goal is to have a lightweight and comfortable backpack and equipment that doesn't weigh much. Consider eating dehydrated food as it is light. If you don't take these suggestions into consideration you'll end up hauling a fifty-pound pack instead of a twenty pound one for miles and miles. Trust me, the weight on your back will make a difference with each step. Backpacking isn't for everyone and may be difficult to pull off with your family in tow, especially if this is the first camping trip.

CAR-CAMPING

This is pretty simple. All the things you need are in your car and you drive to the campsite. You unload a popup shelter or tent and a sleeping bag. You might have kitchen items to cook by the fire or you may choose to eat at local restaurants. Whether you build a fire or not, you're experiencing the version of camping that works for you, so embrace it. I highly recommend this for your first outing, especially if you have a family.

SUPPLIES FOR BACKPACKING VERSUS CAR CAMPING

Personally, I think there's a good chance you will enjoy the outdoors. Which means that eventually you will end up with two setups—one for backpacking and the other for car camping. Backpacking provisions need to be ultra-light, whereas supplies for car camping can be bulky and perhaps less expensive.

ADVANCING FURTHER

You've got to right-size your trip with what your family wants so that camping is a successful experience. You may need to take several simple car-camping trips before progressing further. Or, your group may be content with this simplest kind of adventure. But, maybe it grows into more. Perhaps add a campfire to the next trip, or cooking over the open flame, or a longer more involved hike. The trick is that if it's a family thing, go slow and let everybody ask for more so they don't feel forced. I have found the biggest objection about camping is that people don't want to get out of their comfort zone.

CAR GLAMPING

Which means bringing every creature comfort from home. There are different levels of glamping. Honestly, sometimes I feel like I glamp when we go to our place in the mountains because of the luxury items we haul with us. The over-the-top items we could bring are a super-big tent, which we'll talk about later, a flat screen, an Xbox, a generator, maybe some gilded throw pillows. I'm sure you've heard of the glamping sites where you can go live in a tent that's a lot like your house. They can even have air-conditioning!

ECONOMY GLAMPING

Connie and I go "economy glamping." We bring a ten by twenty feet tent. My choice would be much smaller, but it's all about compromise. I want her with me and happy, so we've figured out what

Connie makes camping comfy

each party needs to feel comfortable for a weekend. That includes an inflatable mattress. We don't wear shoes in the tent, which keeps it much cleaner. There is a small area designated for shoes and dirty clothing. We also have a cozy spot to sit down. These are things we do to make the clean up easier and the space more comfortable. Given these conditions, Connie will gladly come camping with me.

Our big tent

With a big tent, you have room for an air-mattress. In fact, a big tent will usually allow everyone to sleep under the same roof, which goes a long way to a good night's slumber for all. The more comfortable you can make camping for your loved ones, the better the chance that your kids will want to have epic, hard-core adventures in the future.

CAMPING WITHOUT CAMPING, IS IT POSSIBLE?

What works for your family? You can always stay in a hotel or a bed-and-breakfast that's close by to your activities and then do day trips. I'll argue that you're not camping per se, but those day hikes and discovering waterfalls, will still get you outdoors. It will allow you to spend quality time with loved ones and set yourself up for those priceless moments with your family. If staying in a hotel and having day time adventures works, then do it!

WHAT WILL WORK FOR YOU?

As you can see, there is a vast range of options for camping. Are you an RV kind of guy where you plug in at a campsite with power and air-conditioning and running water? Perhaps it's going to be something simple, where you have a tent and minimal equipment and eat at restaurants. Or maybe you'll go for something in between. There's no wrong answer as long as you're getting everyone outdoors and create those family memories.

WHAT ARE MY GOALS AND INTENTIONS?

As you can see, the camping experience can span

quite a range from a tent and a sleeping bag, to many of the creature comforts of home. Ask yourself:

- Where's your comfort zone?
- What do you want to accomplish?
- How much effort do you want to exert?
- How much do you want to spend?
- How much time do you want to be at the site?

GETTING EVERYONE TOGETHER TO CREATE MEMORIES

The goal is you want to get your family outdoors and allow everybody to have a great time. Depending on if you choose an RV, a pop-up, or a tent, may or may not affect whether or not you have that priceless moment. I think with an RV you're a little more separated from things. But people have different comfort zones. If the only way you can get your people to camp is to rent a pop-up or an RV for the weekend, then do what you need to do. You're achieving some of your goal, everybody's having a great time, and you're creating family memories, which make it all worth it.

DON'T FEEL PRESSURE IF CAMPING IS NEW TO YOU

There's no pressure to be Mr. Outdoors. Because if you're the kind of person who has never been in the wilderness before, no one would expect you to build a fire with flint and steel and some cotton you pulled out of your pocket. Feel free to use matches. Keep it simple when you build your first fire, and maybe even your tenth. Later on we'll talk about some of these other skills. But, my goal here is to give perspective on your different options.

Most of my camping experiences revolve around family trips or Boy Scouts. As a result this book really focuses on family camping. However, the same principles, skills, and knowledge apply to a single person or family. Maybe you are a single man or woman who wants to experience camping for the first time. You could be a widow or widower, or newly divorced. There are many people in lots of different situations that head out to enjoy camping. This book spends a lot of time talking about family interactions and considerations, but the skills and knowledge apply to a variety of life circumstances. If you don't want to go by yourself, then consider joining an outing club. It's a great way to go with a group and enjoy the camping experience.

BUILD UP YOUR SKILL SET

You may need new outdoors skills. Or perhaps it's time to teach those techniques to your kids or spouse. You never know when you need to build a fire. Your car may break down in a place that has no cell service and the only thing to keep you alive overnight is to build a fire. Does this happen to everybody? No. But, the simple ability of building a fire could be a lifesaver. One reason to continue to camp regularly is to keep our skill set sharpened. This gives peace of mind and boosts confidence. Learning outdoor knowledge improves self-reliance that translates to other areas of life. These regular camping trips build a happier, well-adjusted, better-prepared-for-life family member who is more available to partake in those priceless moments.

It's not a question of how rugged someone is. The question is what they want. Some people at different points in their lives simply don't want to spend the weekend working hard outside doing camping stuff. Sometimes you want the fun component and not the work part. So instead of a tent and open flame cooking, they might choose an RV and restaurant food. Or perhaps they'd rather do something at home that weekend.

COMPROMISE

There are trips when Connie doesn't come because I am hunting and I'm fine with that. Sometimes it's nice to be on a solo trip, or a trip with the guys. It's an opportunity to go with a smaller tent and do different activities. The point is to keep the perspective that there are a lot of ways to get a win out of camping—backpacking, economy glamping, hunting backpacking are just three. They all have their pluses.

FIRST TRIP COULD BE A SOLO ONE

If you are unsure about camping for the first time with the entire family, then consider just going solo, or with your spouse. Then bring the kids on the next trip Camping can be enjoyed in lots of different scenarios from the whole family going, or individuals without children going solo (or with a group), or situations where only one parent takes the kids.

The key is to figure out what works for you, at this time in your life, with whoever is going camping with you. Don't feel pressured to be Mr. REI, because that won't make you happy and it isn't what your loved ones are looking for. Kids are seeking quality time spent with Mom and Dad. Your spouse is looking for the same thing. Leave your pride and ego at home. Camping is about those priceless moments.

Small tents are functional

THREE

FINDING PRICELESS MOMENTS

Remember the Meme on Pinterest that I talked about in the first chapter? It showed a Prius at the top of the image, and at the bottom a Jeep in the desert sitting on the crest of a hill, in front of a sunset. A guy and his kids are in the Jeep enjoying the sun setting in this majestic place. The closing message of the meme said, "Your kids will never, ever remember you getting fifty-five miles per gallon. However, they will remember the night you watched the sun set over the mountains." Let's talk about some camping basics today.

WHY GO CAMPING TODAY?

Because there will never be another today. In the Prius Meme, the point is that *things* don't matter, *experiences* matter. Perhaps you can make a daily drive fun with some singing or frivolity. Or perhaps ride to the top of a mountain to watch a sunset. Those are the priceless moments to chase after. I encourage you to get out and enjoy life. Not everything has to be constrained, and I think in many ways that's what camping is all about.

Daughter having fun

DON'T ALLOW CHALLENGES TO GET IN THE WAY

When you consider camping, there can be challenges: you might get rained on, it could be extremely hot or cold, the bugs might be extra annoying, dry kindling may be hard to find, etc. But, at the end of the day, the goal is to *build memories*. There are only so many opportunities to go camping with your children or your spouse or even take a solo trip. Right now it seems as though you have all the time in the world, but you really don't. Your kids will be in college or active in other things before you know it. So grab those moments while you can.

THE EXPERIENCE MATTERS, NOT THE STUFF

Someone who had a very nice late-model sedan asked about my Jeep. He indicated that if only he had an off-road vehicle, he would try camping. Why go camping if you can't go trail-riding, he said. *That's the wrong attitude.* True, driving on thirty-five inch tires with a four inch lift and a bunch of modified stuff is great. It's nice when you're riding around on a spring day with no top and you've got no doors. But you can still create those priceless memories by rolling down your windows and opening your moon roof.

PERSEVERE

The trick with camping is that you can find yourself in a rugged situation, for example it might rain the whole weekend leaving you nothing to do but play cards in the tent, or after rain from the first night all the kindling is wet and you can't start a fire, maybe an animal got into your food supply and now you have nothing to eat. It doesn't matter what happens, the secret is in how you handle the situation.

Don't give up, persevere. Sometimes camping makes no apologies. Your skills might be tested, but I am going to promise you that you will still have opportunities, even on those off weekends, of making solid memories. You might be sitting around the campfire or hiking or hearing the coyotes howl or watching the sun set or building a fire with your child—those priceless moments can't be bought so grab a hold of them.

KEEP A LOOK-OUT FOR MEMORIES OF A LIFETIME

Keep your outlook fun and positive because you can't predict when memories will be created. But trust me, your kids will remember and they'll tell their children about these special times one day. Just put yourself in a good situation to have those moments. They may occur in your Prius getting forty-five miles per gallon because of the song you sang. Or perhaps when you're sitting on top of the mountain and out of your element as you watch in fear as a bear ambles by. Be available and put yourself in situations to achieve those priceless moments.

Coming up, we're going to look at convenient, low-cost, low-pain, and low-suffering ways to be in a good situation to discover joy. By attaining that joy, you get those memories that will live on because you taught the next generation skills. And one day, your kids will not only pass along the skills to their children but will share their childhood priceless moments around a roaring campfire.

Connie's amazing breakfasts come with a smile

FOUR

IMPORTANCE OF TRADITIONS

While camping, one thing you'll end up developing are traditions. Some are big, some are gigantic, some are small, but all are valuable.

HOW TO BUILD TRADITIONS

You can either purpose to repeat activities, so after a few years they grow into traditions. Or, traditions can happen by accident. Something may work well once, so you repeat it. By the tenth time you realize you have a tradition. Keep in mind that when you do something that is comfortable and enjoyable, you'll keep doing it. You may find that it is important to your family to go camping on a certain date or a particular place because it brings back special memories and there is an expectation that you're going to make more good memories—that's a tradition.

REPETITION BUILDS TRADITIONS

I'll give you an easy example. There's a restaurant in Winston-Salem, TJ's Deli, that Connie and I tend to stop at when we're headed for the mountains because it's on our way. They have awesome, homemade sandwiches and to-die-for fried mushrooms. Now, don't get me wrong, this isn't a fancy place, more like a hole-in-the-wall, but the draw is the food and the tradition. We order the same meal every time, a gigantic sandwich and fried mushrooms on the side—I always save some of the mushrooms for the remaining drive. Even when we travel with friends, we stop there. Every time.

Is having a meal partway to your destination part of camping? No, but it can be part of the entire camping experience. When we head west to camp, we usually work our departure around stopping at TJ's Deli for a meal, which we both look forward to. The detour helps break up the trip and I think the tradition is nifty.

Another tradition we have is camping at Troublesome Gap every Memorial Day weekend. We are so predictable that friends call to ask if we are going this year. Those calls made me realize traditions can even spark a camping interest with friends.

TRADITION LOOKS DIFFERENT TO DIFFERENT PEOPLE

You may never go to the same restaurant twice, but

you may have a tradition of stopping at some restaurant on your way to the camping site. You may never camp at the same location, but you may set your supplies up in the same order every time. Or you'll always be sure to have a campfire. Or roast marshmallows.

You could lean towards more open spaces because you like to throw your daughter up in the air in the middle of a grassy field. Or perhaps you like to take a morning walk right as the sun is beginning to rise and dew still licks the grass blades. Maybe one of your kids is an early riser who likes to get up with you and help build the morning fire, which is a teachable moment by the way.

PRICELESS MOMENTS

You guessed it, when a tradition is created, most likely a priceless moment will as well. Look for those traditions, spur them along, and allow them to happen. Some occur organically. Some we purposefully build. You can't force them, but you can encourage and grow and build them.

KEEP UP WITH TRADITIONS

When camping with others, they're watching. So if you always have a ham sandwich with onions the second day for lunch or you always have s'mores the first night over a roaring campfire, then your family may be disappointed when the activity doesn't happen. Usually these traditions are special camping experiences, not something you normally do at home. Some traditions are hard and fast, and some of them aren't. You'll just have to work that out depending on your family.

ANYONE CAN START A TRADITION

Sometimes you'll do the most obscure activity with your kids, maybe throwing knives into an old stump or forging your own path in the woods. It may not make an impact on you, but your child doesn't forget and wants to do the same activity the next time you go camping. *It's usually the simplest things.*

Perhaps you take your family on a spectacular hike and see breathtaking scenery, but the thing your kids remember from their day is the mound of soil behind the apple tree they created dirt castles from. Whenever you get the chance to interact with your children, do so. Even if it's making dirt castles under a canopy of low-lying tree limbs. Those are the moments to grab and revel in.

If you are single and reading this book, then you can still build great traditions while camping with friends or family, or going on a solo trip. If you are divorced or widowed, a camping trip could be just the thing you need to get out of your day-to-day rut and create wonderful new experiences. While I'm spending a lot of time talking about family camping, there are still many ways to enjoy a trip while single, divorced, or widowed.

BE FLEXIBLE

If you're into schedules, that's great. But keep in mind, if someone in the family is enjoying an activity, put that hike off for an hour. If there's rain in the forecast, consider doing an activity closer to the campsite. Agendas don't matter, the memories and time together does.

STORIES GROW OVER TIME

Kids remember events. Some of those stories grow like fish that you caught. You know the story of an angler who catches a twelve inch fish and by the time he tells the story about six times, its two feet long. Well, sometimes memories are that way too. Sometimes they're precise; other times they're not even close. But, what matters is the memory.

I'll give you an example that's not camping related. When one of my daughters was in elementary school, I began going to school and having lunch with her once a week. Kids won't be young forever, in fact there may come a time when they don't want to spend much time with you. Anticipating this, I made a point of making that weekly meal a priority. A number of years into this tradition, my daughter noted I'd been coming to have lunch with her every week since whatever grade. She enjoyed it, I enjoyed it, and so it remained a tradition, a thing between just the two of us. She valued the time I carved out for us. Over the years when she'd tell the story, she'd share we'd been lunching together longer than we actually had. Should I correct her? No. Am I trying to encourage her to be inaccurate? No. I guess the thing is it pleased her that we had lunch together once a week. And so, it was a big deal that became a bigger and bigger part of her life. And her nailing down exactly when we started doing it really didn't matter. What mattered was how appreciative she was because we were making lifelong memories.

INTERESTS CHANGE

Your kid's interests will change over the years. Be flexible. Something that is important to him this year may be boring four years from now. This means your camping trips may change. The important thing is to give your kids attention, relate to them, and listen to what they want.

At some point you or your kids will look back and be thankful you hiked every waterfall trail in North Carolina, or made s'mores every night around the camp fire, or took the time to find a thick enough branch to make a walking stick the first night of each trip. Those were traditions and you enjoyed yourselves and made memories. But, there may come a day when your kids decide they'd rather spend time with their friends and that's okay. You need to roll with it. You've spent years developing a set of experiences and memories that you can share and remember forever.

Continually ask questions and listen to see what the

people in your family want to do this year and next. If we can be flexible and go with the flow as interests and needs change, then we have the chance of keeping the tradition of camping alive and the opportunity for creating more memories. In fact, a lifetime of them.

Also keep in mind that *your* interests and capabilities change. Maybe you used to be able to hike ten miles a day when you were younger, but now perhaps four is your max. Or maybe you used to hike only difficult trails, but you've learned that moderate means success. On the other hand, if you want to push yourself then take a long hike. Maybe you used to hike moderate trails, but after hiking a challenging trail you realized you have the capability to hike longer and more difficult trails, so push yourself and revel in that accomplishment. If you are camping solo, then this may be a good time to enjoy the fruits of your physical fitness efforts with a long challenging hike. Alternatively, taking your athletic, teenage kids, on a difficult hike may be something they really enjoy. Just keep your capabilities and stamina in mind so everyone, including you, can enjoy the physical challenge.

QUALITY TIME

Whether it is a yearly guy's trip, or a monthly trip with young kids, or maybe a romantic getaway with your wife, the important thing is to be free from distractions and spend quality time with loved ones. If you have more than one child, each parent should try to spend concentrated time with individual kids. You may find your children consider this quality time a tradition. Now, note that tradition for traditions sake is worthless, unless you are accomplishing something important.

TRADITIONS ARE USUALLY SIMPLE

Many times traditions aren't bound up in spending some ridiculous amount of money, but are instead simple. It may be somewhere you ate, and spent the majority of the meal laughing. It may be playing in the mud behind the apple tree. It may be hiking a specific trail that you've hiked every year for twenty years.

For example, if your wife or child is asking to go on a particular hike again, you need to figure out if they want to go on a general hike or a specific trail and for what reason. What do they really want? What's important to them? Ask questions and dig. Because they may be looking for the smiles, laughter, and love they felt on a past hike. Maybe it was just you and them on that trail. Perhaps Mom wasn't there, or maybe Dad wasn't there, and was just the two of y'all. That's the moment you'll realize there is a new tradition of going on this hike, perhaps just the two of you. And it'll be a special time. Then you make your plans based on this information and how you can make it work.

DON'T TRY TO PLEASE EVERYONE

Depending on the age of your children and how many you have, satisfying only one for the next ten minutes might be your only option. Sometimes everybody's in tune and sometimes they're not. In those challenging moments, you may want to break up your group. If you have two children with two *totally* different interests at the moment, maybe Mom goes with one child and Dad with the other. Breaking that up gives you the opportunity to pursue those varied interests. And there again, build those great memories. But, maybe you have a situation where everybody wants to do something together. You can figure it out even if it's not always easy.

PLAN, BUT DON'T PLAN

One tip I suggest is make a list of activities available for your location. If you don't plan, but instead wait until the last second, generally whatever you wanted to do won't happen. Say there's a national forest right down the road; maybe you pack into the car and go there to experience the wonder of it all. Perhaps there's a body of water close by so you get into a canoe or a row boat or a paddle boat. That can be fun as well. Keep in mind though, you may have camping trips where what everybody wants to do is sit by the fire and relax. And all of a sudden, it may explode into a hiking trip, and then they go back to sitting by the fire. So, planning is great, but also be flexible and see what happens. But, don't forget the simple things like running around in the woods to just explore. You can also make a game of the mundane activities that it takes to put together a campsite—like, accumulating stones to edge the fire or gathering kindling and firewood. My point is to make time for organized hikes or rafting trips, but leave gaps available for exploration and inspired play time. Sometimes the simplest and least expensive things are what we remember.

ALWAYS KEEP BUDGET IN MIND

I have found it's not the amount of money you spend; it's the fun, fellowship, and relationship building. Keep in mind, if you spend money on something and it stresses you out, everyone will pick up on the stress and fun diminishes. Perhaps you can do something that costs close to nothing and still enjoy yourselves. I have found the best trips right-size your activities with your budget, your physical capabilities, and everyone's expectations.

In the process of talking with folks about this book, I'm not surprised to hear they have such fond memories of camping as a child. I hope you can find your own traditions, and develop those priceless moments everybody will cherish for a lifetime.

FIVE

WHAT TO DO WHEN YOU ARE CAMPING

Let's tackle where to go camping and what to do when you get there.

PICKING A CAMPSITE

If you choose a campsite at ten thousand feet overlooking half the state, well, that's awesome. But there's probably not a lot to do up there unless you're into epic hiking or rock climbing or bouldering. If your family's not, or you have young kids, you will not meet with success. If you want views and relaxation, then this is the place for you. But, if you want to be near water you're probably going to be closer to the valley.

One of the advantages of a campground is that other

people are around and they may have amenities. There might be a game room with a pool table or a foosball table or air hockey table. There might be a lake with canoes and a place you can fish. Also, there are usually other people around so your kids may be able to find someone to play and have fun with. A place like Bear Den Campground, in Spruce Pine North Carolina, is a good example.

Another campground choice is to camp near where you want to explore. For example, Asheville has the Biltmore Estate and art galleries and loads of shopping. Perhaps that's part of the camping experience. You camp where you can be close enough to Asheville. Say you have lunch in downtown Biltmore, then walk through a bunch of art galleries. That makes everybody in your family happy. In the afternoon, you go back and sit by the campfire. Another day you may have a totally different experience where you spend a day at Sliding Rock. And the next day you hike waterfalls on Mills River, or you hike up some mountain, or visit the Carl Sandberg home or Moses Cone estate. The list is endless. And all these activities are within a thirty-minute drive of the campsite you chose.

Now the downside to a campground is that you've got other people around, which means you're not going to have that "I'm alone and there's no one within fifty miles of me" experience. The flipside is the higher the concentration of people, the more there is to do. I recommend checking what's available in that national forest or that campground or that state forest, and then check what there is to do in the neighboring towns. Usually if there is tourism, there are other things to do besides camping.

CHECK REVIEWS, MAKE A PLAN

I recommend choosing your campsite based on the activities you want to do and the places you want to go. Also, always check reviews and look for a variety of activities. Another idea is to get in the car and drive around. It all depends on whether you like to plan and schedule ahead of time or figure it out as you go.

Some historical sites can be fun for even young children. For example, Moses Cones Manor, off the Blue Ridge Parkway, has several thousand acres with gorgeous views, a lake, and paths. That's a nice choice for young and old!

Everywhere you go is different. Some hikes that have spectacular views may be hard to get to, so you have to ask yourself is it worth it. There are many shorter and moderate hikes that have equally amazing views, so investigate and ask around.

NEED A FISHING LICENSE?

When you think about fishing, you need to check on the fishing license in that state. In North Carolina you must have a license to fish anywhere other than private property. So, if you plan on fishing, check out the license issue ahead of time.

NON-ACTIVE PURSUITS WHILE CAMPING

A non-active experience is when you're sitting around the campfire, reading a book, napping, or spending time on your smart phone. It could also be where you've camped on the top of the ridge at six thousand feet, and the sun is rising across the mountains, and it is the most gorgeous sunrise or sunset you've ever seen in your entire lifetime. This is something you can experience without leaving the comfort of your camping chair. Maybe even your tent, depending on which way your tent faces. Passive experiences aren't bad, they are just different. There are times when non-active is the way to go.

ACTIVE OPTIONS

Hiking, rock climbing, horseback riding are options. Water options include: canoeing, paddle boating, fishing, rafting, or kayaking. Consider taking a lesson in rock climbing, horseback riding, kayaking, or rafting class. If you're in Western

Hiking at Red Rock Park in Nevada

North Carolina, slide down Sliding Rock—trust me it is so much fun! Another fun spot is The Historic Orchard at Altapass, which allows you to go apple picking, shop, eat ice cream, and sometimes they even have live music.

Depending on who is in your camping group, you may decide to go out to lunch, shop in the next town over, walk through an art gallery, a zoo, or museum. Consider your audience. The point of each trip is to have fun and have everyone want to go on *another* camping trip.

You might want to do a ropes course, where you're fifty foot up in a tree, climbing. Keep in mind that it's safe because that's the only way these companies will be in business tomorrow. For example, the Nantahala Outdoor Center will teach you a short course on how to raft. And then they'll put you on the river, and you can enjoy a more family-oriented day of rafting. If you want to go big water, go to the Gauley; it's not for young kids but it's awesome for adults.

PASSIVE VS. ACTIVE, OWN IT!

I want to give you an example of my lovely wife. We can be in the most amazing spot and Connie is completely content sitting by the campfire in the afternoon, reading a book. And I'll say, do you want to go for a hike? And she'll look at me and say, no go ahead without me. She is completely content. We've been doing this camping thing awhile, so Connie knows what she likes. I'm not going to force her into something she doesn't like. She enjoys the somewhat passive experience a lot of times when we go camping. So during our down-time when we could be hiking or biking or canoeing, she'd rather read. But when it comes to meals, we work as a team.

Fishing and relaxing

WHAT IS YOUR STANCE ON A SMART PHONE WHILE CAMPING?

When your kids get to be teenagers, they may be tethered to their phone. Now, this is your fight to fight. But, camping is a great opportunity to set some new house rules. Use your judgment because if you completely take something away that they're used to having, maybe they respond well to that, maybe they don't. You don't want anger and frustration to be the imprint of your camping weekend. You need to figure out what works for your family. It may be tough for someone to give up unless they really, really want to. I think that's important to keep in mind. There are different ways to approach that. You could leave the phones at home. You could have them an hour a day. You could have a morning and evening time where phones can be used, but otherwise not at all. I really think it depends on the situation and how busy you're going to be and where you are and what personalities you are dealing with.

MUSIC VENUES ON THE CHEAP

If you are near Marshall, North Carolina, every Friday night at the train depot they have music. Everybody's doing covers for the most part, think Johnny Cash tunes. Mostly local people attend this community gathering and everybody has a great time singin' and pickin' and grinnin'. There is a small donation to get in. Kids will possibly hear music they don't hear otherwise, and see a different culture that is totally different than what they're used to.

Another good example of musical venues is Shindig on The Green in Asheville, every Saturday night. That's you and a couple thousand of your closest friends on the grass at City County Plaza enjoying bluegrass music sitting in your camping chair. Many of these events are family-oriented, but do your research first. Check the venue, the type of music, use good judgment. A lot of these gatherings happen regularly and they are really cool. They are a great way to break up your camping experience.

OTHER "CIVILIZED" ACTIVITIES

Maybe go listen to a few hours of music, or go to an arts and crafts festival. Get away from the campsite. Give everybody a little touch of home, so they feel "civilized" again. I think that's important because you don't want camping to become this horrendously intimidating epic-or-nothing type adventure. Instead ease into it so everyone has a positive experience. Make sure to only push the comfort zone so far, and that way everybody wants a return camping trip. Maybe the next time you push a little further.

CAMPFIRE RULES

Think about setting what I call "truck rules." Guidelines that may not be acceptable in the home, but in a truck or camping, they are for your family. One example we have is that in a truck you can make bodily noises that wouldn't be socially acceptable otherwise. It's about letting go of some finer points of decorum so your kids don't feel like their sitting in the dining room surrounded by china. This is the time to let everybody unwind a little bit.

You've got to figure out what's appropriate for your family. I'm not suggesting that all of a sudden you allow your kids to call you by your first name. I'm saying, if a kid farts you laugh about it; you don't fuss at him. If they spill beans on their lap, you laugh. And you don't quit laughing. Because you're making a precious moment; relish these times.

I'd also like to remind you not to overindulge in alcohol. First, you're out in the woods and if someone gets hurt and no one can legally drive, there's no way to get to the emergency room. Second is that you're out in the woods and you need to keep your wits about you. If you're going to drink, drink lightly and be smart.

Sometimes relaxing is the best by the fire

LET KIDS BE KIDS

Camping is the perfect time to encourage kids to enjoy outdoor activities, not just organized ones, but impromptu fun. If they want to play in a creek, let them! Assuming they know how to swim and are aware of the dangers, keep an eye on them from a distance and allow them to be kids. This is a great opportunity to give them clear guidelines and begin to let go. If you're on this gigantic place of open woodland, forest, desert, whatever, tell your kids the extent of where they can go, keep track of them. But let them go be kids. Sometimes they need that unstructured play.

Now, obviously, if you have a three-year-old and they want to play by the lake, you need to be there. You must keep an eye on young children, but if a ten-year-old wants some latitude, now's the time to give it to them. Always use your judgment as a parent, but keep in mind they've probably never had the kind of freedom they are looking at during this camping trip. They will not get these opportunities in the city and maybe even in a lot of suburbs.

So, ask yourself what unstructured activities you can encourage your kids to partake in. Near water, or no? Climbing trees with thick, low branches? Fishing is always fun, but you can keep it simple by using a cane pole with natural bait. You don't have to be a well-equipped fisherman to have a good time. Sometimes the simplest things are the better.

I have found that when you get equipment in the way, the equipment occupies your attention, not your kid. Be attention heavy to your kids, because when you get that brand-new five-hundred-dollar fly reel and you're in four hundred-dollar waders, you're worried about that stuff, not helping your kid cast that rod and reel.

KEEP THINGS IN PERSPECTIVE

I think perspective is important. Part of the reason I'm throwing these parenting ideas out there is because there are areas I've messed up. Sometimes I wonder if I should have given my little kids more freedom and less structure playing when we camped. I feel they would have enjoyed the experiences more. I hope you can learn from some of my missteps so that your camping trips are chock-filled with priceless moments.

WHAT WILL EVERYONE REMEMBER?

Will it be the hike, or the view, or the campfire, or the messy S'mores? Perhaps it'll be the game room or snack shop at the campground. Who knows, for twenty years they may talk about that game room and snack shop with their sister and the amazing ice cream they got their every year.

Everybody has a different take away from all these things and sometimes it's tough to put yourself in other people's shoes and understand what they will remember. Who knows, they might remember the time they saw a bear, and that might lead to them to study bears in college so they can be a forest ranger. Or it may just be a story they fondly talk about.

My recommendation is to try different things over the years. Personally I don't like being cooped up in a car so I think the more time you can spend out of the car is probably good. If it takes two days to drive somewhere and you're there for one day, and it takes two days to drive back, I don't think you have a winning plan. If you really want to go to that location, consider flying. But you need to ask yourself what your comfort zone is.

WONDERFUL MOMENTS CAN BE UNSCRIPTED

Some of the memories my kids have about camping are surprising. Some of them have been totally unscripted and wonderful moments that I didn't even see coming, but, you know, the kids said let's do this. So, we went and did whatever on a lark, and then, you know, an hour later, it's like Wow!

A great example of a wow moment is a last minute hike. My daughter and I took a last minute hike and the view across this mountain top field with the fog rolling in was totally amazing. Words could never do the view justice so I won't try. If we hadn't gone, based on her suggestion, we would have missed out on an amazing moment. Other times I planned things well in advance that turned out great. It's kind of tough to predict that ahead of time.

The trick is planning the trip and getting to the campsite. That's where the winning occurs. You may have camping trips that are difficult. If it rains all weekend, consider playing cards in the tent, or go to the nearest town and go bowling or play laser tag.

Don't feel like your plan is set in stone, roll with the punches. The point is to be together, have fun, and make memories. The tent could fall down and you think it's a total disaster, but because you laugh about it and handle the situation with patience and calm, *that* is the good memory your kids take away from the trip. Who knows, they may talk about it for years to come! So remember, your attitude can make or break those precious moments.

UNSCRIPTED DECISIONS CAN LEAD TO FUN!

On a funny note we were camping one time, and a thunderstorm started rolling in. We'd been hiking all day on Mount Mitchell, when we returned about three quarters of the people at our campground had already left. The people who were still there were packing furiously. Since we had been off-line all day, I asked why everyone was leaving and discovered the weathermen were predicting a thunderstorm worse than any they've had for a hundred years was going to hit in about four hours. We had already planned to be away that weekend, so we decided to stay and ride it out. Guess what, my daughters and I had a lot of good memories riding out Tropical Storm Bob in a tent. To this day we laugh about that weekend and carry sweet memories around it. We kept ourselves safe, we had a solid backup plan so there was no real danger. Bottom line, I think roll with the punches, enjoy it, plan out the activities and let's go camping!

SIX

TYPES OF TENTS

A tent keeps you dry and warm and comfortable. When you're outdoors if you're dry and warm, you're alive. When a tent leaks, you get wet. Once wet, it's hard to stay warm; almost impossible if it's cold outside. I'm not trying to state the obvious. I'm not attempting to scare you. But, if you've never been camping before, I want you to realize how important the tent is.

Family camping is where you leave your home, drive to a campsite, unload your stuff at the campsite, pitch your tent, set up your kitchen, and then you enjoy being outdoors.

ULTRA LIGHTWEIGHT BACKPACKING TENT

One extreme is an ultra lightweight backpacking tent. They are generally dome-style tents. Those have aluminum poles and or fiberglass balls or carbon fiber or partially carbon fiber balls.

For me, I prefer my REI quarter dome, four-pound-ten-ounce backpacking tent that I can pitch in the rain or snow in about ten minutes, no matter what. Even though it's a wonderful tent for one person, at six-two, 225 pounds, the tent's tight. Though, if I'm going camping or hunting, I don't need a big tent.

If it's cold out, a smaller tent will keep you warm because you've got less space. The tent helps keep you warm by trapping still air and keeps water and snow away so you are drier. An added benefit is that as you breathe you're going to heat up the air. The general rule of thumb is the tent adds ten more degrees to the performance of your sleeping bag, assuming you have a pad underneath. So a forty-five degree bag is comfortable for sleeping at forty-five degrees. If you're in a tent, the same bag is good for sleeping at thirty-five degrees.

A BIG TENT FOR LUXURIOUS CAMPING

My wife and I tend to work from the opposite ends of the spectrum, I consider myself a minimalist, but she is not. I like that Connie likes to go camping, and she picked a tent to allow her to be comfortable. And if she's comfortable, we'll likely go camping again. So, my wife bought a large tent that cost two hundred and twenty-five dollars. My small REI tent, which is a higher quality, was about three hundred dollars (but I purchased it on clearance, so I paid less). Now remember I took that REI tent camping for fifteen years, which was a great value. I doubt we'll enjoy the same lifetime out of Connie's ten-by-twenty foot tent.

Some people say a large tent is not camping. I disagree because camping is getting out and enjoying the outdoors. If you want to go backpacking, you can't bring a ten-by-twenty foot tent. If you're going to go car camping and you have plenty of room in your car for the tent, you can. So, one of the things Connie does when we head to our place in the mountains—there's no backpacking involved; it's pure car camping—she puts a liner down on the floor and then rolls out some type of bamboo thing to keep the tent floor clean for the week, we set up an air mattress and a fold-up chair.

Keeping things organized makes the trip easier and less work

I have to admit, she creates a luxury space. I can stand up in the tent; even dress standing (which I can't do in my REI backpacking tent); there's also a chair to sit in. Camping is very comfortable in Connie's setup. If it rains, we've got a place to put a table inside to play cards. Not only does Connie like comfort, she also enjoys organizing. Trust me, keeping things organized in a quarter-dome tent is practically impossible. But the setup Connie has come to enjoy works well because it is spacious, clean, and organized.

I will caution you that the larger the tent, the more difficult it is for one person to easily manipulate. Our giant tent is a handful; it's big, heavy, and probably weighs about thirty pounds. So that's a consideration. Make sure you bring something that fits your abilities. If you're not strong then keep that in mind when selecting camping equipment.

THICK CANVAS CABIN TENT

The other end of the extreme is a cabin tent. A cabin tent is what you see on one of these shows where someone goes hunting in Alaska and they're going to be there for a month. The tent is one room and has a wood stove. The fabric is thick canvas and they're about twelve-by-twelve or ten-by-ten. Kind of what you would see in a movie about the Civil War. There is a front door and they used to be popular. Now you see these heavy duty ones in very cold climates, like Alaska. This generally isn't what you're going to take family camping.

SELECTING THE RIGHT SIZE FOR YOU AND YOUR FAMILY

My wife's gigantic tent works well for our situation. It takes longer to pitch and is tougher to put up, but when we're done there's plenty of room. The tent came from Walmart, isn't the highest quality, is a twelve-man tent, and works for us. If you're gone for a week, whether it takes ten or thirty five minutes to pitch the tent doesn't matter, the time spent will be worth it.

Tents are rated for the number of men who can lie down in them, not sleep comfortably. A two-person tent is super tight for two adult males. But for a couple who is just sleeping, it can be cozy. Consider giving yourself enough room to spread out and think about whether you want living space. Also, consider whether you want to crouch or stand in the tent.

Be cautious with how much money you spend on a tent, but at the end of the day, if this is your first camping trip and you may never go again, consider purchasing a large inexpensive tent. Be careful, because if you snag it on limbs or pull and tug on it, it can easily rip. But if you're careful and take good care of the tent, then you'll get a longer working life out of it.

With a quarter dome tent, I'm more or less climbing out on all fours. Whereas with the big tent, I unzip the flap and duck my head down a little bit and walk out. So consider the amount of headroom you feel you'll need and what mobility restrictions you may have.

Tents come in all sizes

Don't forget, there are many options in between a quarter-dome and a ten-by-twenty larger tent. The trick is figuring out how to make your family comfortable. Remember, the goal is to have a great time so you go camping again.

Generally priceless moment happen when everyone is comfortable, well-fed, happy, and everything's going easy. So, make sure you set yourself up by rightsizing your tent.

SELECTING THE RIGHT QUALITY TENT

Tents from REI (I use them as an example because they have quality products) tend to be higher-quality than Walmart tents. At the same time there's absolutely nothing wrong with going to Walmart to purchase a tent, especially for your starter tent. As you know by reading this book, you're going to have other things you may want to buy to go camping.

The downside of a cheaper tent is the lower quality and possibly the shorter lifespan. A higher quality tent is more expensive and lasts longer. Until you start using the tent a lot, just about any tent should work well as long as you take care of it properly.

If the tent you purchased falls apart on your first

camping trip, return it to the store. I bought one from Sears one time and it leaked on the first trip so we brought it back for a refund.

WHAT TO DO WITH YOUR NEW TENT

The first thing you want to do is set up the tent *before you go camping*. Go out in the backyard on a beautiful day, and pitch your tent. Read the instruction manual. Let whoever is going on the trip help. Maybe set it up two or three times until you've got the procedure down pat. Because you never know what the conditions of the campsite will be. It could be dark or raining, you can't predict, so you want to be prepared.

Wherever you pitch your tent, make sure the ground is free of sticks and rocks or anything that can cut the fabric of your tent.

If your tent offers a foot print option, buy it. A footprint is basically an extra ground cloth for under your tent. Many times it'll clip into the structure and become an additional layer that's held in place with your stakes. Those are awesome. Footprints help protect the bottom of your tent and help the tent from not leaking as you have two layers instead of one.

If your tent doesn't offer a footprint, what I usually do is take a tarp or some type of waterproof ground cover and place it under the tent. The important part is to make sure the ground cover is *completely* underneath the tent.

Otherwise, when water hits the ground cover, it may simply force the rainwater to run underneath the tent and stay there which can cause leaks.

TAKE DOWN THE TENT

I know I already talked about this in a prior chapter, but let me reiterate that if you can, take your tent down dry. If you can't, you need to find a place when you arrive home where you can open it up and let it dry for a few days. If the tent stays in the bag wet and all curled up, it will mildew. Mildew does two things: it's going to smell horrible, and will make the tent start to leak. Storing your tent dry will help prolong its life.

SEVEN

FORGET SLEEPING BAGS, THINK SLEEP SYSTEM

Even the best sleeping bag will have fairly limited usefulness without support. Given that, let's talk about the broader topic which is your sleeping system.

YOUR SLEEPING SYSTEM

A sleeping system is made up of four elements. The first is the tent, which prevents rain and snow off of you. But, it also keeps wind away. When you're outside and the wind is blowing, you feel colder. So, a tent keeps cold air at bay and traps static air in the tent. The ventilation a tent provides is also important in hot, humid weather. We'll talk about types of tents in a later chapter. Hammock tents, commonly referred to as Enos, are another popular option. However they are nice for solo trips and require trees the right distance apart. Hammock tents are best for more advanced campers, not a family trip.

YOUR SLEEPING BAG

The second element in the sleeping system is either a sleeping bag or sheets and blankets. A sleeping bag keeps you warm by creating tens of thousands of small pockets of air. There are a variety technologies for doing that— down, Hollofil, Quallofil, or a simple polyester fill. Keep in mind these options come in different price points.

SLEEPING BAG TEMPERATURE RATINGS

The temperature rating on a sleeping bag is the lowest outside temperature where you are still comfortable. The rating assumes you have an insulated pad under the sleeping bag and are sleeping in long underwear. This also won't account for the cooling effects of wind chill, but your tent protects you from the wind. It is very important to keep in mind that some people sleep warmer than others and the temperature ratings of sleeping bags vary from manufacturer to manufacturer.

A ten degree bag will be very warm in the summer, while a fifty degree bag will be very cold on a thirty-five degree night. One way to extend the temperature range of your bag is to use a sleeping bag liner. A liner is good for approximately ten additional degrees of warmth. You can also use the liner by itself when it is really warm out.

However, for your first trip you may want to consider sheets and blankets on an air bed instead of buying sleeping bags. Another option is to borrow sleeping bags from friends or family. You may also be able to find used camping equipment. You can wash a used sleeping bag before you take it camping.

THE DOWN OPTION

You pay for quality and technology in a sleeping bag. The technology used is often designed to keep you somewhat warm, even if the sleeping bag gets wet. For example, a down bag is compact, lightweight, and tends to be warm. That makes it the perfect option for backpacking; but when wet, a down bag is pretty close to useless. The key is to keep it dry while it is in your pack and when it is spread out in the tent. The need to keep a down bag dry and the additional cost are reasons to avoid a down bag for your first trip. If you're embarking on your first trip and you plan to car camp, it may be wise to start with blankets and comforters that you have at home. That way you've lowered your initial investment. Once you enjoy your first camping trip, you can consider purchasing additional pieces for future endeavors.

THE QUALLOFIL, HOLLOFIL FILLED BAGS

Bags that are designed to keep you warm even if they get wet are Quallofil or Hollofil filled. They are made up of a variety of fibers that have different ways of maintaining a space of trapped air. Sometimes those fibers are hollow and there may be other strategies; but the idea here is even if that sleeping bag gets somewhat wet, you're going to keep *some* of the warmth, which could be a lifesaver in a difficult situation. Also, either of these bags will dry quicker than down.

THE POLYESTER OPTION

When we think about family camping, the least expensive option, polyester filled bag, comes to mind. These bags are inexpensive but have a limited temperature range. You'll want to make sure your bag is rated to a temperature at least 10 degrees below the lowest temperature you expect to see at that location. Polyester filled bags don't stay warm if they get wet but their low cost can make them an attractive option for your first car camping trip. Instead of an inexpensive sleeping bag, consider saving more money and bring sheets and blankets from home.

TWO-PERSON SLEEPING BAG

Another option is a two-person sleeping bag. You can purchase them at Bass Pro shops or other sporting goods stores. Often the two-person bags are very warm and comfortable. There are rectangular one-person bags that can be zipped together to form a two-person sleeping bag.

We've got a couple of those. And those are awesome. You know, they're covered with duck cloth on one side and flannel cotton lining on the inside. They've got a lot of fill material. And they're really warm. I think we spent eighty bucks each at Bass Pro Shops. Though, I would never take that backpacking because it's monstrous and heavy. But, for car camping where I really don't have a weight and space constraint, it's really comfortable because you get in that sleeping bag and it's soft and warm. That sleeping bag is keeping you warm by trapping small pockets of air around your body. Those pockets of air act as insulators.

ADD A PAD UNDER THE SLEEPING BAG

The third part of your sleeping system is an insulated pad. The pad underneath your sleeping bag is a necessity. Keep in mind you don't have to go out and buy everyone 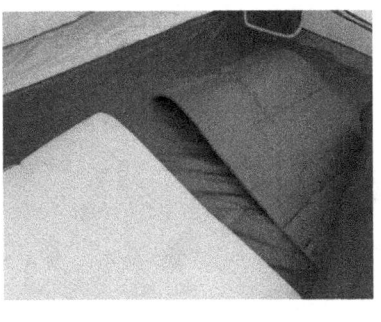 a three hundred dollar bag just to go camping for the weekend. Don't think of the sleeping bag as a completed product, think about the system you're using to sleep with. For example, a simple system for backpacking would be a sleeping bag, a tent, and a pad underneath you. The pad is used for thermal insulation, comfort, and keeps you from getting cold. Your body weight compresses your sleeping bag, which loses the effectiveness of the insulation. So, if you don't have a pad underneath the sleeping bag, you're going to be very cold. The concept is that air will be trapped above you but not below, therefore precious heat is lost into the ground.

PADS AVAILABLE

There are several different pads available at various price points. You can choose either foam, self-inflating, or an inflatable pad. A self-inflating pad actually inflates on its own when you roll it out whereas you have to blow up an inflatable pad. I've used the inflatable and foam, and they both work great. The difference with both types of inflatable is that when not in use they flatten down and are small and lightweight.

The inflatable pads and beds are really awesome as long as there's no leak. The risk with a leak is then you are sleeping on the ground. You may be able to temporarily patch an inflatable pad, if you can find the puncture. If the leak is occurring in the area where the pump attaches, then it may not be possible to repair the inflatable pad or bed. It's difficult to patch an inflatable pad in the best of circumstances. If the patch mostly holds then you may get part of a night of sleep before the pad or bed deflates and you are sleeping directly on the ground. Foam pads, as opposed to inflatable, don't fail, are fairly inexpensive, and last a long time. Though they take the most space of all three, they can get wet and still get the job done. Don't forget that with car camping you can use heavier and more bulky items that tend to cost less and last longer because you only need to lug them from the car to your campsite. On the flip side, if you are hiking several miles into the woods, you would want to go with one of the inflating pads as they are significantly lighter and much less bulky.

If the weather is warm, perhaps fifty degrees or higher, you probably won't need a pad under your air mattress. However, the foam pad is a great backup in case your air mattress leaks or for some reason you aren't able to pump it up.

POSSIBLY ADD AN AIR-MATTRESS UNDER YOUR SLEEPING BAG

The fourth and final part of your sleep system is to add an air mattress between the pad and the sleeping bag. You will still need a pad if it is cold to retain heat. If you are backpacking, you wouldn't take an air mattress. If you are car camping, the air mattress makes your sleeping experience in the tent much more comfortable.

Another neat thing about an air mattress is that it can do double duty. If you invest in one for camping, you can still use it in your home for company. When camping without electricity, you'll need to invest in a D-cell battery pump, or a pump that runs off the cigarette lighter in your car, to inflate up the mattress. You can also use a hand pump, which is less expensive, it just takes longer to inflate. I will say check your air mattress before you leave home because if it has a leak, you have a problem. And usually you'll have to pump them up every day and a half or so while camping. Keep in mind that the older you get, the more you might appreciate the feel of an air-mattress. It will keep you a foot off the ground and allow you to get up and down easier. So we age, an air-mattress may be a way to extend your ability to camp longer throughout your life.

The air mattress, or inflatable bed, is inexpensive and come in sizes as large as queen. Since you are car camping for your first trip, the size of the bed when it's packed up isn't usually a big issue. Make sure that your an inflatable bed actually fits in your tent before you get to the campsite. I know I keep mentioning this, but setting up your tent and air mattress at home, before you leave to go camping, is always a great idea.

One caution I have for you is to carefully explain to everyone to not plop down on an air-mattress. If that air mattress fails it's going to be a long night sleeping on the ground which is pretty hard.

HOW AN AIR-MATTRESS CAN FEEL LIKE HOME

We have a queen-size air-mattress, a single rectangular sleeping bag, and two single bags that are very large. Given those tools, my wife will lay a bedspread or a blanket on top of the blown-up air-mattress and then a fitted sheet over that. Then, Connie will put a regular sheet over that and lay the single rectangular sleeping bag on top. Finally, she'll zip the two single bags onto the square one on the bottom—creating a roomy homemade double sleeping bag. This setup is very comfy and warm and feels more like the bed at home than a slick sleeping bag on a backpacking pad. This homey feeling makes the sleeping part of camping more comfortable and more like the bed at home. This is a win for everyone because a good night's sleep helps make for a good next day.

For your first camping trip, you can make it simple and place a double sleeping bag on top of the air-mattress and call it a day. Of course, you can also do this with a blanket or a comforter, and then there is no need for a sleeping bag. Be cautious with using comforters from the home because many times they are dry-clean only or too large to fit in your in-home washing machine when they get muddy or dirty. On the other hand, sleeping bags and blankets can go through the wash with no worry. Note that down bags require a special soap and drying method to keep their loft. It's not hard, you just need to follow the instructions. You also want to minimize the number of times you wash your sleeping bag.

STILL USE A PAD IF YOU HAVE AN AIR MATTRESS

The air mattress has you up off the ground and provides *some* insulation, but it's this giant pocket of air, so it's not as effective as a pad, which contains lot of small pockets. That big air mattress has limited insulation and can allow you to feel the cold ground below. So, when the weather is cold, make sure to include an insulated pad between the mattress and the ground. This will help keep you warm. Depending on the size of the air mattress you may need to put two insulated pads side by side.

RECAP OF SLEEPING SYSTEM

So that gives you a system, possibly for a low cost. Your linen closet contained the blankets, comforters, and sheets, if you choose not to purchase sleeping bags. You may have already owned an air mattress or can borrow one from a friend or neighbor. Now, at minimal cost, you're prepared to go camping. And you're extremely comfortable. By doing this, you can get an idea if your family enjoys camping. If they do, then you can begin to invest in more products to keep yourself warm and comfortable.

PLANNING CAN MAKE ALL THE DIFFERENCE IN ATTITUDE

If you follow my steps and plan for a quality tent that won't leak, a pad to keep the cold and wet from your bedding, an air-mattress for comfort, and warm coverings to snuggle under—whether it be a sleeping bag or blankets and comforters—everyone at the campsite will be warm and comfortable. The system will feel much like their bed at home. Everyone will get a good night's sleep because you've created this amazingly satisfying environment to sleep in that is similar to their bed at home.

THE FIRST NIGHT

For me, a lot of times I don't sleep well the first night because I'm out of my normal element. But there's a big difference in levels of not sleeping well. For example, if I'm laying on the ground on a pad in a mummy bag, I'm probably going to, that first night, sleep less than if I'm snuggled up to my wife on an air mattress, all warm and everything's wonderful. It's a lot easier on that big, thick air mattress to get a better night's sleep that first night.

SUBSEQUENT NIGHTS

Usually, the second night I sleep pretty good, it's the first night that gets me. I think that means I'm mentally and emotionally in a better position the next day to be friendly and loving and kind, and not grumpy because

I didn't get enough sleep. Given this, don't feel like that there's anything wrong with bringing the comforts of home with you.

ENCOURAGEMENT

The big thing is that I want to encourage y'all to get out and enjoy the outdoors. By all means, if you've got to do a little more "glamping", or glamorous camping, than just playing camping that's just fine. It's all a process. Each trip puts you one step closer to having the skills you need for the next level. It also puts you one step closer to say a backpacking trip, or some more adventurous type camping. Or maybe you stay in the glamping stage forever, that's fine as well.

AFTER THE CAMPING TRIP

I only wash a sleeping bag when I have to. If it's muddy or dirty or smells, it needs to be washed. I ALWAYS air out sleeping bags well after a trip. I have a rail above the stairs that allows me to leave the sleeping bag open while hanging over the rail. You can also just leave them open on the floor or on your bed. Make sure your sleeping bags are dry and clean before storing. If you let it mildew, it is very difficult to get that odor out. Don't roll up your sleeping bag tightly for storage, or put it in a compression sack, instead store in a dust free environment or loosely in a bag. That will help prevent the sleeping bag from losing its loft, and the warmth the loft helps create.

CAN I SAY...

You are on your way to developing a love of the outdoors, along with the skills and sense of freedom necessary for camping. If you want to push yourself with each trip, go for it! Otherwise, enjoy the outdoors in whatever set-up works for you and your family.

These tips on the sleeping system are great ways to keep everyone comfortable and give them a good night's sleep. I think that helps the overall camping experience. So, get on out there and enjoy the outdoors while camping.

EIGHT

CLOTHING FOR CAMPING

On your first trip, I'm sure you'd like to avoid going out and spending a lot of money on expensive gear, but keep a couple of things in mind. If you're in a commercial site where there are many other campers around and you're ten minutes from a bustling town and you have no plans to venture anywhere else, then you don't need to purchase a lot of camping clothes. On the other hand, if you'll be in a remote area far from others, then you have to be prepared for anything.

KEEP IN MIND THE HIGH AND LOW TEMPERATURES

When we are home, we are used to a seventy-three degree house during the day and sixty-eight at night. When you're outside camping, you can easily see a ten, twenty, thirty, forty, fifty degree swing over the course of the day. I will say it depends on where you are. Usually the largest fluctuations occur where it's dry, because there's less moisture to trap the heat, as well as at higher elevations where you find a bigger temperature swing at night. Say it's seventy during the day, and forty at night. That'd be a thirty degree difference. We have seen swings from 85 to 30 many times in the mountains, especially in the high desert.

STAY WARM, STAY DRY

The way to remain alive is to stay warm and dry. It's very important to keep yourself in a situation where you *can* stay alive, because the number one killer of outdoor activities is hypothermia.

You can freeze to death at seventy degrees. If you are wet at seventy, you're not going to be able to maintain your body heat. If you are wet at seventy in the shade and the sun is about to set, you will also struggle. Keep in mind that very young children or older people can't sustain their body heat at some of these temperatures if they don't have the appropriate clothing. In those cases, hypothermia is a real threat.

RULES OF THREE

You can survive three minutes without oxygen, three days without water, and three weeks without food. There's a little bit of a variable in that equation, but it's pretty accurate. In three days you're going to be suffering from massive dehydration and your body's going to start shutting down. In three minutes you're going to suffer from oxygen deprivation and brain damage can begin.

HOW A 9-1-1 SEARCH CAN START

Generally, if you are lost you're going to be rescued within two or three days. And if people know where you are, you're probably going to be found in twenty-four hours. But, let's say it's three-thirty in the afternoon, and your kid goes for a walk and gets lost. You don't realize your child is missing until five-thirty when Mom's calling everyone to the campsite for dinner. It may take awhile to discover a child is missing. There may be calling and searching before you realize your child is lost and you call 9-1-1.

By the time rescue personnel arrive and gather the facts, it may be dusk. Depending on weather conditions, they might wait until morning to search. One of the dangers rescue teams have is the risk of walking over uneven terrain at night. It turns into the rescuer needing rescuing. Many times when someone is lost, they won't be found until the following day because of darkness, so the more prepared they are, the better chance they'll survive.

STAY DRY. I MEAN IT.

If you are conscious and dry and warm, then you'll be

fine. You can live without food and water overnight. You may feel cold, but you'll survive. The key is to remain dry.

What if it rains? Either huddle under the canopy of a large tree or gauge what direction the wind and rain is landing and put yourself in a situation where you can remain as dry as possible.

If you get wet in a rainstorm, use the rays of the sun when it reappears to

allow your clothing to dry.

EXAMPLE OF WET CLOTHING IN COOLER TEMPERATURES

When your clothing is wet, your body loses heat very quickly. The cotton T-shirt or hoodie you are wearing is useless, because the water conducts the heat away from your body, and cools you off. So now all of a sudden, its say seventy degrees, but your body can't maintain that temperature because of the heat being lost.

Your body maintains a temperature of about ninety-eight degree. Let's say the air's seventy, and your body's producing energy so maybe it's seventy. But, once you are wet you're not okay. It is now dark and you have to spend the night in a place where you don't have a way to dry off. When wet you lose more energy than you're creating; this is when hypothermia could begin to kick in. People think *that would never happen to me*, but unfortunately hypothermia is one of the big outdoor killers.

HYPOTHERMIA DEFINED

Your body needs to keep organs at your normal body temperature. If your body is losing heat, the first thing to happen is your extremities cool off. Your fingers and toes get cold; as long as you don't develop frostbite or the digits don't freeze, then not a huge deal. It's not uncommon for your skin to reach fifty degrees.

But, eventually you lose so much heat that your body starts to get cold *inside*. Your organs are not comfortable with being at those temperatures. So, in protection mode, your body begins to reduce the amount of blood flow to the skin. One way your body saves heat is to tighten your capillaries. But, your internal organs—liver, lungs, heart, they are all starting to get colder and eventually shut down. Next, your mental capacity goes down as well which is why people may start hallucinating. In advanced stages of hypothermia, they may stop talking or may not be able to communicate any more. At that point you have a serious medical condition. The only way to fix it is to warm the person up.

HOW QUICKLY DOES HYPOTHERMIA SET IN?

If you are lost and wet and can't maintain your body temperature; hypothermia will set in. If you are a young child or an older person, it is more critical. The colder the air is the quicker hypothermia starts.

For example, say you fall into the Bering Sea which is about thirty-two degrees; you have about two minutes before hypothermia sets in. Or say you tumble into a seventy degree lake, you have about three hours. The basic concept is if you don't warm up, you're going to die.

Let's say you aren't wet. Or you are wet but the temperatures aren't extreme, you are in for a long night. Hypothermia might not set in, but it will be a miserable night. It would also be a reason for someone never to go camping again. So, it's more than just keeping track of your kids; its preparing them because things can happen. But, there's hope. Read on for tips to prevent hypothermia and getting lost.

SIMPLE THINGS WE CAN DO FOR SAFETY

Help the people in your group understand where they are and how to return to the camp site. Also, train them in what to do if they become lost. If they don't have equipment or proper waterproof clothing, there are still a number of things they can do.

Remind them to stay dry and warm, and make sure they know *why* this is important. Another thing is don't move around after nightfall without illumination as it is easy to fall and injure yourself. Next thing you know you'll be lost and hurt. It's best to sit down after dark sets in.

You can also teach the people in your group about the

terrain. If you're camping halfway up a mountain, give them a landmark they can go to, that way you'll know where to find them if they are lost. For example our place in the mountains has two peaks; one is on our property and the other on the neighbors. Everyone knows if they are lost to walk uphill until they can't go anymore, that is where we can easily find them if darkness sets in and they don't return to camp. Think about whether there are terrain features you can give simple directions around, so even a child can understand how to get to a place where it's easy to find them.

EXAMPLE: NOT LOST, JUST HURT

Let's say you are out hiking alone, and you fall. You've broken something and you can't make it back to camp. No one can hear you yelling and darkness is settling in. If you've left camp prepared, then you can rough it for a night with the pack I'm about to tell you about.

EQUIPMENT EVERYONE NEEDS

Knowledge is power, but when camping, proper equipment can rule the day. If everyone is prepared with a pack when they leave the camp, that one simple thing can help prevent bad situations.

One item everyone should have is a waterproof jacket. The best kind is one with breathable fabric, for example Gore-Tex, but there are other good ones. If it is warm and you don't need a jacket, tie it around your waist or stick it in your pack so you are prepared.

Of course, you should have water with you and some type of food, perhaps a Cliff bar or trail mix. It's also smart to have a flashlight. If it's going to be less than eighty overnight, bring a hoodie with you.

It's really nice if you have a piece of plastic you can use to make a shelter. It's also wise to have a way to create or build a fire. Both those aren't necessarily essential.

Those are the basic things to put in your pack. Now you've filled up a small backpack. But, keep in mind many backpacking backpacks have a removable top section where you can store these items, so when you go for a side hike, you drop your bag and take these other things with you and you're good to go.

DON'T PANIC

If someone does get lost, the first thing they should do is sit down, take a deep breath and think about where they are and where they've been. It may be that if you can keep from panicking, there is a simple solution to return to camp without a lot of difficulty. If you're panicked, you might be fifty feet from where you need to be; but you head off in the wrong direction and two miles later you're farther away from where you need to be. Things like roads and rivers and unique trees or bushes are all solid landmarks to help people find their way back to camp.

DON'T RELY ON ELECTRONICS

Any electronics or something with batteries eventually dies. If you give someone a handheld GPS receiver or a compass and a map, they can probably find their way back, assuming they have the skills. A GPS is handy, but the batteries on a map and compass never die. Knowledge weighs nothing. Being able to find your way with a topological map and compass is a guaranteed way to know your way home. You can receive basic orienteering skills in an afternoon, time well spent.

With a GPS, you can set up a waypoint and use the GPS on your phone. Then you can compare the point where you're camping to what your phone says, or the handheld GPS receiver, and make your way back to camp.

You still need to have the ability to survive on your own without technology, because batteries can die, or maybe you lose your signal. GPS signals can be hard to find in the mountains with trees or in a heavily forested area, even. So, it's important to keep in mind that the phone is a wonderful thing, but there are a lot of places where it might not work.

A non-cellular GPS can have issues because of trees and terrain as well. GPS can fail for a lot of reasons. That's why it's so important to have self-reliant skills in case the batteries die or there is no signal. Your kids may look at you funny when you ask them to take a handheld GPS receiver, but it might save their life if they have to spend the night somewhere.

HOW PREPARED DO YOU NEED TO BE?

Now this goes back to where are you in your camping experience. If you have a one-year-old and you're not going to leave the campsite, then you probably don't need to spend two hundred dollars on a waterproof jacket for everybody.

I'm a big believer in preparedness, so I'm probably a little more prepared than most. But if this is your first trip, with people and help nearby, then keep it inexpensive. Take some sweatshirts, take whatever gear you've got, maybe an umbrella, and keep it simple and economical. Don't have a thousand dollar credit card bill. And don't go in debt to go camping. Just have what you need if you get lost.

On the other hand, if you're going to the middle of Wyoming and you'll be a hundred miles away from the nearest help, that's a totally different trip and you need to be prepared.

Many lost individuals are found very close to camp. Some have died from hypothermia, as close as ¼ mile from safety. So always be aware of your surroundings and how to find your way home. Do use proximity to others and safety as an excuse for not being prepared.

IN GENERAL, WHAT TO WEAR

Because it gets cool in the evenings, carry a hoodie for everyone. Depending on weather, bring a rain coat or umbrella. Also, since you'll be outside all day, wear sunscreen or a hat, your skin isn't used to having sun beating on it all day.

Now I don't have any hair so I have to wear a hat. On the other hand, my wife has a lot of hair but she normally wears a hat. Another item to think about is sunglasses; they can keep the sun out of your eyes.

Wear comfortable clothing, shorts during warmer weather. Consider whether you might come across poison ivy. If you are allergic to poison ivy, bring an EpiPen. Bring anti-itch cream. Depending on where you are, you may want to add bug repellent as well. These are basic things to make you more comfortable.

You need to have rugged footwear, unless the plan is to exit the car and set up camp and not leave, then you don't need to invest in expensive boots.

HAVE FUN

The goal is to keep everybody warm and dry sitting around the campfire. That makes for happy campers and you'll have those wonderful moments. Keep track of everyone in your group and help them understand what to do if they do get lost so they're crystal clear of what to do. Train your campers!

NINE

BUILDING A CAMPFIRE

If you grew up in the country and split your own logs you can skip this. In this chapter we'll talk about the four types of wood. Going from smallest to largest, the first is tinder, then kindling, then wet wood, and finally dry wood.

TINDER

Tinder is lightweight and burns fairly hot for a short period of time. You use it to light larger pieces of dry wood. That's really the concept of a fire—you start with small stuff that's thin and ignites easily and at a hot temperature, so that you can then light something a little bigger and then a little bigger, then even bigger. Tinder is the easy-to-light fibrous stuff. It's not going to burn long. Usually if it's easy to light and puts out a lot of temperature it's going to burn pretty quickly.

Tinder is basically a fire starter and comes in a variety of forms. One form is off a log from a long-ago-dead tree. You strip back the bark and you'll find a fibrous and lightweight layer between the bark and the tree. That layer is easy to light.

Another form is newspaper or fire starters you can buy from the store. You can make your own fire starter with a combination of sawdust and wax, put the mixture in a paper egg crate. There are other ways to make fire starters, just check the Internet. There's a lot of ways to start a fire.

I will warn you to stay away from leaves as they usually put off a lot of smoke and not a lot of heat, instead you want to look for soft, dry material.

KINDLING

Kindling is broken or dead branches and other forest litter whose diameter starts from the size of your thumb on up. Unfortunately, not all branches around a forest are dry.

If a branch is dead, (i.e., no leaves, no green growth) that tree is no longer able to provide nutrients and water to the limb, so it's going to be dry. If it's appropriate where you're camping, you can snap off a dead branch and use the tips to start your fire.

Squaw wood is where you have dead wood that is up

off the ground. For example a fallen limb stuck between two branches, or maybe it's still attached to the tree and it's about to break off, or it's lying across a couple limbs and has broken off. Since it isn't on the soil, it'll be drier than branches sitting on grass or dirt. That's the kindling you are looking for because moisture from the terrain hasn't been saturating the timber, especially if it hasn't rained lately. It will tend to be drier than the wood lying directly on the ground. Dry wood makes it easier to build fire.

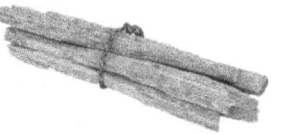

Fat wood kindling is a great firestarter

If you're out in the western part of the country, humidity is extremely low and it's not really a big issue. If you're on the eastern part of the country, or say you're in the Appalachian Mountains, humidity can make starting a fire tougher because that wood can absorb moisture from the air. A bigger problem is when wood absorbs moisture from the ground. Damp wood is hard to light.

DRY WOOD VERSUS GREEN WOOD

The drier the wood the quicker and the hotter it's going to burn. Wet timber is harder to ignite and you'll find it burns longer at a lower temperature. Our tinder lights our kindling, then as the fire builds you'll use bigger pieces of wood. That kindling may be the squaw wood or branches you know are good and dry.

CHECK LOCAL ORDINANCES

In some areas you aren't allowed to pick up dead wood. It depends on the status of the forest you're in. So collect small pieces of kindling from your backyard before you leave home and bring them with you, maybe in a bucket with a lid to keep it dry. Break them up into a bunch of small pieces and you've always got that available.

MAKE SURE THERE ISN'T A FIRE PROHIBITION IN THE AREA

Sometimes it gets dry in the summer and there will be a prohibition against campfires. When the park, or county, decides there is a chance for forest fires, they may ban campfires. Always check before you leave to go camping.

HOW TO BUILD A FIRE

When you start your fire, tinder is going to be underneath very small pieces of wood. One way to think about this is how a tree grows. You have a trunk and branches, and the branches branch into twigs, and eventually you get out to the tip where the buds are. This smallest wood tends to be less than an eighth of an inch in diameter.

If you have a fire starter and you put it underneath an eight inch diameter log, that combination is not going to catch the log on fire. Building this fire is a matter of starting and working through these stages: easy to ignite; very small diameter tinder-type stuff; up to kindling; up to what we'll call firewood.

Build a fire with tinder at the bottom, then twigs about an eighth of an inch in diameter, then sticks about a quarter of an inch in diameter. The tinder lights the twigs, the twigs light the sticks. As the fire grows you add bigger and bigger fuel, but take it slow or else you'll snuff the fire out. When you get to where the kindling is the size of your thumb, then you start looking for small pieces of dry wood about two times your thumb.

My point is to slowly build up your fire by increasing the size of the timber. At some point you'll notice burnt pieces of ember dropping down and creating a bed of coals. This is the stage where if you've gone ahead and split some logs into pieces about an inch by an inch square, by whatever the length of the wood was, maybe 16 inches, then you can start putting those dry logs on. This wood is more substantial than the twigs, so they're going to burn hotter as they catch on fire. At this point you can add bigger logs.

You may also want to consider building a square chimney out of your smaller split wood. Then you can start your fire down in this hollow chimney. This will trap the heat from the tinder and progressively larger pieces of wood and help to protect your incipient stage fire from wind. This approach also warms up the split wood and eventually ignites the larger pieces.

Later in the evening you may want to throw on a big log as a backstop. It will sit there and start to catch on fire. It's going take a long time to ignite, but when it does, it's going to burn for a long time, which is awfully nice while enjoying the campfire.

Once you have a bed of coals, you can start introducing some green timber because it burns slowly. The advantage is you're not going to have to add wood as often. Though your fire will not get as hot, it'll burn longer. That's the point in the evening where you're looking to sit around the campfire. If you're going to cook something for a long period, sometimes small pieces of green logs will help stabilize the cooking temperature. Keep in mind, if wood is very green, then it won't burn well and you will have problems keeping your fire burning. Avoid that frustration and enjoy the fire by using dry timber.

SCRAPS OF WOOD

Once, when we were camping in Bear Den Campground in North Carolina, right off the Blue Ridge Parkway, I met a cabinetmaker who saved his sawdust and wood scraps in a bucket with a lid. Over time, the bucket full of kindling became bone dry. He used that to build a fire which worked really well. So, if you're a wood worker, save your scraps. Break them down into small pieces, and use that to start your fire.

BUCKETS FOR KINDLING

You can obtain free buckets at Walmart or any grocery store from the bakery department. They may have a bucket full of icing they're working from. A lot of times they'll give you those buckets and they'll have lids. Are they waterproof? No. Are they water-resistant? Yeah, for the most part. So, you can probably keep your stuff dry.

Or you can go to Home Depot or Lowes and purchase three-gallon buckets in the paint department for about three dollars. They also sell lids that snap onto the bucket. Home Depot has started carrying Omega Lids with an O-ring which makes it water resistant. Put your woodworking

Bucket for kindling

scraps or kindling in this bucket and screw on the lid, now you've got dry material to build your fire. Though it will take room up in your vehicle, if you're planning to build several fires it sure makes life easier. Depending on where you're camping, you may need to bring in all your wood.

WARNINGS

Do not go to bed or walk away from a fire until it's out. Out means you can put your hand over where the coals were and the area is cool. Fires can re-catch and you can start a forest fire.

Once you start a campfire, you have to tend it. You can't go away for thirty minutes because something could go wrong. The fire could spread and you start a forest fire. Always watch a fire. Be careful. It's a great tool. Like any tool, fires deserves respect and a little practice.

USING AN ACCELERANT

Keeping a source of tinder and kindling with you is awfully handy. Another thing you can do is use an accelerant. So, let's say you have lighter fluid and you want to build a charcoal fire. You can soak your wood in it for maybe ten or fifteen minutes before you light it. If you don't give it time to soak in, the lighter fluid will sit on the surface and when you ignite it, there'll be this giant *poof* of a flame and then it'll be done and not a lot will catch on fire. Optionally, kerosene or diesel work well.

The challenge is whenever you use an accelerant, you introduce risk. When you light this thing, it's going to ignite quickly and burn hot. Be careful, you don't want to burn yourself or start a forest fire. Let's say you've got a bundle of wood about a foot by a foot by a foot and you pour a gallon of white gas on it and you let it soak for an hour. When you light it, it's going to give you this little mini fireball. That wood is going to burn for hours, you'll have a hard time putting the fire out. And so, as a result, you want to avoid using an accelerant.

I will admit I've had times where I've been forced to use an accelerant. Either it was pouring rain or for some reason I was having a hard time keeping the fire started. I've used kerosene or white gas, but I will say I've had some negative experiences. So, I recommend staying away from an accelerant for camp fires.

For example, if you were to hold the white gas container in one hand while you light the fire, when the lid fell off the white gas container, you would understand the unpleasant experience. Alright, I was seventeen at the time and stupid. Learn from my mistakes and stay away from accelerants. Thankfully it was a small bottle of white gas, one of the ones we used for a backpacking stove. We got in a hurry, wanted the fire to light; threw some white gas on the wood, picked up the lighter, unbeknownst to me gas was on my hands, and there was this little bit of a boom, and it scared me! I dropped the gas container and the next thing I knew fire was everywhere because the white gas ignited. It was bad idea. I learned a valuable lesson.

If you choose to use an accelerant, go easy. Ninety-nine percent of the time you can build a fire successfully with what you have. If you're in the Appalachian

Mountains and it's been raining for two weeks and the fog is rolling in and everything you have is soaking wet, then you're going to have to make your own decision. I would encourage you not to use an accelerant, just because of the risk. You know, lighter fluid works fine on charcoal because charcoal absorbs the fluid readily. The wood may or may not absorb the accelerant as readily and so you can have a situation where it's on the surface of the wood and not absorbed. Be careful.

EXCEPTIONS

With a rocket stove, you're going to stay with fairly small sticks the whole time, and you won't need a stick bigger than three-eighths of an inch. That's the advantage of those; they're very efficient. If you use a Kelly Kettle, you're going to use small twigs the whole time. You want to have a big stack of small twigs and just slowly feed the fire. The difference with the rocket stove and the Kelly Kettle is that you get hot water quickly. The downside is they need constant feeding of fuel. The very good thing is that you really don't need much fuel to heat your water. A small box of small twigs can get you through several pots of coffee or bowls of oatmeal.

With a campfire you get up and add some fuel or branches or a log, every five or ten minutes when you get it going; maybe longer if it's really going well.

But with a rocket stove or a Kelly Kettle, you're going to feed it constantly. If you walk away, it'll just go out, because there's just not a lot of fuel there and not a lot of thermal mass.

MORE COMPLEX FIRE ARRANGEMENTS

A Dakota Hole or some rocket stoves rely on the fact that the heat is hottest at the tip of the flame or slightly above the flame, and so you build a fire in a teepee style. There's a bunch of styles you can use— square or teepee to name a few. You could even use the Swedish fire log approach, which is really cool. You could even use a Swedish fire log approach, which is a little different and unique. Some people out west use Dakota holes. I've never built one that way, though it seems kind of cool. We've built a half Kiva before on a windy trip. There are a lot of specialized ways, but most of the time you're sitting around a campfire, and you build a fire inside a little ring of rocks.

WRAP UP

The best way is to use a fire starter. Use tinder. Use kindling. Start small with your fire. Make it bigger. You definitely want to keep in mind that the heat is going to be the hottest above the flame, or at the top of the flame. Successful fires push hot air across the wood.

YouTube has videos on how to build a fire. There's tons of stuff written about how to build a fire. And so, it's something you want to figure out, what fire building approach works best for you.

Roasting marshmallows over the fire

TEN

HOW TO DRESS IN LAYERS

When you're active, your level of physical activity determines how much heat your body generates.

At the same time, the weather can change quickly, so the amount of clothing you may need to keep you warm varies over the course of the day, and over the course of your activity.

If you're really active, let's say you are on a long hike, then your exertion is creating a lot of body heat. You want to reduce the amount of heat you're maintaining in your body so you stay at a comfortable temperature. Getting sweaty means you have wet clothes, which don't keep you warm later. Staying comfortable, no matter what the weather, is critical to enjoying the trip. The clothes you wear are a huge part of your comfort.

Year round you need to be concerned with staying

dry, in colder weather, you need to make sure you stay warm.

REGULATE YOUR BODY TEMPERATURE WITH LAYERS

When you become warm, you can take off a layer. When it gets cold outside, you can add a layer. A lot of times people don't realize how easy regulating your body temperature is and how much it contributes to your comfort outdoors.

For example if you go from a seventy degree house in the middle of winter to a twenty degree car, you'll have on a thick coat to stay warm. Once the car warms up, you take off the coat. The coat kept you warm until the car heated up, and then you shed the outer layer. On the flip side, if you're outdoors and you have the same thick coat on in a chilly climate, and let's add that you're moderately active—you may need half of the insulative value your coat can provide. With common sense, you'd unzip it which means your arms and back would stay warm and your chest cold. The best way to regulate your body temperature outdoor is to dress in layers.

In the above example where it is cold out and you are exerting energy, you might want to dress in multiple layers, so you take layers off and on during the day as you exert energy and feel warm, or as you move into shady areas or stop for a break and feel cooler.

You also need to be concerned with moisture; in this

case rain or snow. A common approach is to have a waterproof or water-resistant outer layer.

BASE LAYER

The base layer is usually a wicking or poly fabric. This is the layer that touches your skin. Silk is the best fabric because it pulls moisture away from your body. When moisture touches the skin, you're not as warm and you get cold. Those materials pull dampness away so it doesn't wick the heat directly away from your body. There are two parts to the base layer, the shorts (or long johns if it is cold) and the top.

You'll notice I threw out the names of different fabrics you'll see in these situations. One of the materials I didn't mention was cotton. The problem is when cotton gets wet; it's going to be cold. Wool has a certain amount of natural warmth even when it's cold, and so even a wool shirt that is wet or moist, provides some percentage of warmth without being totally dry. The point is cotton, once wet, won't keep you warm.

WEIGHTS OF BASE LAYERS

They can be light, medium, and heavy weight. What you wear depends on the weather you're in. Most of the time, you'll end up with medium weight. Base layers are often long sleeve, pullover—so think long underwear. The bottoms are the same. Your base layer, top and bottom, both wick moisture away.

THE NEXT LAYER

The next layer may be a sweater or wool shirt. You may choose to have a thicker layer on top of that; and on top of that, you might have your jacket (often water resistant).

CONSIDER YOUR CAMPING EXPERIENCE AND HOW CLOSE YOU ARE TO TOWN

Let's say you are camping close to stores or in a campsite with hundreds of people, and the weather's not extreme, perhaps in the fifties and sixties and seventies, then don't feel like you need to go to REI and buy a bunch of high-performance clothing that's expensive.

WHEN THE QUALITY OF LAYERS MATTERS

As your level of adventure and length of camping trips increase, or you camp during cooler weather, the more you need to think about the quality of your clothing. The outer layer, a waterproof jacket, is critical because keeping water away from your body is the number one thing in staying warm and comfortable. Like I said in an earlier chapter, if you are remote and on an adventurous trip, everyone in your party should have a light-weight waterproof jacket in their pack. After that, having layers you can unzip and take off and store easily, makes it simple to change the amount of clothing you're wearing based on your level of activity and the weather outside.

The other time when higher quality clothing matters is when you choose to camp or hike in remote areas where there's a chance you won't see another soul or perhaps when getting from your campsite back to civilization may take hours. Also, consider your drive to your destination. Are you driving through an out-of-the-way area? When a car breaks down in a remote location and the passengers aren't prepared, especially clothing, for the weather, deaths can occur.

WARNING

I would recommend not dragging your family out somewhere in very cold conditions if they're not used to it because the chance for fun is low. Camping in the snow can be awesome, but you need the skills and equipment and motivation. Keep your first camping trips easy, one where your only concern is for possible rain. Don't make your first camping trip with family in February when it's twenty degrees out and everybody is struggling with just keeping warm. Instead, make your first camping trip somewhere where it's maybe sixty to eighty during the day and forty to seventy at night and everybody will be nice and comfy.

WEARING COTTON IN COLD WEATHER

Most of the long underwear you see out there is actually made of cotton, which, as long as you can stay dry, is fine. If you get wet, then it gets cold. If you're close to the tent, close to other people, then that's probably okay as you can just change into dry clothing. The challenge is if someone wanders off and gets lost; then all a sudden staying dry becomes critical because you may not find them for twelve to twenty-four hours. My point is to use your judgment as far as where you're going to be, and how far away people are going to get from camp or if you go on a day hike.

The other possibility is you go on a day hike, you pick this six mile hike and three miles in rain starts. The temperature drops twenty degrees. At that point, you've got some decisions to make, and hopefully you're prepared and you're not having too miserable of a hike back to the car while you're wet and cold. So there again, it's based on your level of adventure and risk. If you're going to go on long hikes, then being prepared to keep everyone warm and dry is in everybody's best interest.

WHAT HAPPENS IF SOMEONE GETS INJURED

What do you do if someone gets injured? For example, you and your spouse are hiking and you twist an ankle so bad you can't walk. Let's throw in no cell service. You can see how having clothes to keep you dry and warm could be a lifesaver. So, your spouse has to go and retrieve help. You might be talking four to six hours. It might take an hour-and-a-half to hike back, then she needs to figure out where to go, then she needs to go there for help, then medical personnel need to arrive, and finally they have to hike that hour-and-a-half to get to you. You can see how you could be waiting for hours. If you take shock from the injury and add that to the mix, hypothermia is a real threat.

PURCHASE HIGH QUALITY CAMPING GEAR ON CLEARANCE

Just because last year was a different color than this year, it doesn't matter because you can save seventy-five percent. The point is, for clothing you're going to want quality. When you are out and about, it is critical to stay dry because it's easy for something to happen and then you are stranded somewhere for some number or hours, or days, without protection from the elements. Consider buying clothes you'll wear at other times so you make the best use of your budget.

ON TOP OF THE LAYERS, USE FABRIC FOR WARMTH

Dress in layers and then use fabrics that retain their warmth, such as a wool or Quallofil® or Hollofil®. Some fleeces are good about maintaining some level of warmth even if they get wet.

WHAT JACKET TO PURCHASE?

Breathable jackets are the best. Of course the king is GORE-TEX®, but they're expensive. There are other materials that don't breathe quite as well as GORE-TEX® but still keep you dry and breathe to keep you from getting sweaty. I have a jacket I've used for ten years of camping and hiking that's just now starting to lose its performance when it rains. A quality jacket is a staple and a great long-term purchase.

For kids that will outgrow their clothing quickly or drag it through the mud, it's a shorter-term purchase. Consider the length someone's actually going to wear it when you think about how much to spend. As I said earlier, for your first camping trip keep things simple so you're not far from home or not far from other people. When you lower the safety risk, you can get by with lower performance clothes, for example cotton.

HOW TO DRESS IN LAYERS

Dressing in layers means you can peel off a layer as you get warm; peel off another layer as you get warmer or because your activity changes or the weather heats up. When you are more sedentary or the weather cools, you can layer back on.

As the weather gets colder, it's nice to have two, three, four or five layers. But, instead if you've got a giant down coat and you take it off and all you have left on is a shirt, then you may find yourself cold. Whereas if you have multiple layers then you can better match the amounts of clothing you have on to stay comfortable—not too hot, not too warm. When you think about staying warm, sweat is your enemy. For example, if you have on too many layers of socks and your feet get hot, and then sweaty, inevitably they're going to get cold. The same concept works for the rest of your body. If you've got many layers on and you're really active and you start sweating like crazy, take some layers off quickly. Sweat is water coming from your skin and hopefully gets wicked away by the base layer.

Depending on how well your layers breathe, that wetness can take a while to go away and can make you uncomfortable. The more layers you have, the more difficult it is for that moisture to get wicked away and removed from inside your first protective layer of clothing.

Let's jump into an example. Say its fifty degrees outside and you've got three thin layers and you're hiking. Take off the top two layers and put them in your day pack and keep going, they won't weight much as they are thin and lightweight. But if you've got a thick layer on, it may be problematic to fit the thick layer in your bag. The weight of your pack is something to consider.

I know a lot of times I have a Carhartt® jacket that's real thick and real warm, and tough as nails. But sticking it inside of a backpack would be difficult as it is bulky and heavy. Because of that, and because it is cotton, I don't wear it hiking. Instead I wear it when I am working outdoors. Or sometimes when I'm hunting, but when I've taken off my thick jacket I'm around the campsite so I don't need to carry it in my pack. I wear that jacket because it's warm in the winter.

DON'T FORGET YOUR HANDS, FEET, AND HEAD

To stay comfortable outdoors, you want to keep your hands, feet, and head warm. Make sure you've got socks and properly fitted boots to keep your feet toasty. Also gloves for your hands. Don't forget a hat for your head.

However, it's important to note that your body wants to keep your brain warm. If you think about it there's not a lot between your brain and the outside elements. You got a skull and you've got some skin and then, if you're lucky, you've got some hair. My wife, Connie, who has wonderfully long hair, will wear a fleece headband because it'll keep her forehead  and ears warm. In mild temperatures, she doesn't need a hat because her hair keeps her warm. So many hats and toboggans are not good at blocking wind. If it doesn't block the wind and it's windy out, then you lose the effect of the insulation. Now I have no hair to speak of on top of my head, so my head gets cold when I'm outside. When I'm in a sleeping bag I need a hat so my head doesn't get cold. If you're bald, you're going to need more coverage for your head than if you have a full head of hair. A lot of times I'll wear a ball cap until the temperatures really drop, and then I'll wear some sort of toboggan. The good thing is that hats or toboggans don't take a lot of space. You can put them in your bag, carry it with you, or clip it to your belt.

MAKE SURE YOUR LAYERS INSULATE, EVEN WHEN WET AND WINDY

Consider how well each layer insulates when it's wet, as well as windy. Some fabrics, for example, your favorite fleece, might work fine walking from your house to your car on a dry, chilly day. But in severe wind or rain it isn't wind or rain resistant.

Some of the new fleeces, like the soft-shell, are made to keep the wind from blowing through. All fabric is made to trap a thin layer of air close to your body. Your body then heats up that thin layer of air and the heat gets trapped between the clothing and the inside of your body. That's why warmer clothing gets thicker, because you need more airspace. If the wind is blowing, or if you're moving, then all of a sudden you have this wind blowing across your clothing. If your clothing isn't wind resistant, you lose your body heat quickly. Improper clothing ruins the effect of having that warm pocket of air around you.

Some jackets are more wind resistant than others, it really depends on the fabric. Wind resistance can be pretty high when camping, so you may find that you're cold. Let's say you have a base layer and a fleece on top. Or maybe you've got a T-shirt and a fleece over top. And you're cold. And it's windy. If you had a breathable waterproof jacket you could put on top, you'd be much more comfortable than you were before. The point is to keep the wind off of you as much as possible. Once you invest in a waterproof jacket, you'll find a lot of uses for it besides camping.

BEWARE OF CERTAIN FABRICS

Inexpensive fabrics don't do well against your skin. A good example is acrylic. If you have an acrylic toboggan, it's really easy for your skin to sweat where the toboggan sits up against your skin. Cotton is another problem—when the weather is mild, it's fine, but when it gets wet, it's going to be cold. Wool is pretty awesome for keeping you warm. A nice wool shirt can be expensive. So, you'll just have to trade off some of that where-am-I-with-this-budget-wise. Poly fabrics can be great for base layers. Wool may or may not be because it can be itchy.

I've got a long-sleeve pullover shirt that's a wicking material. I've had it for twenty years, and take it camping most of the time. For the thickness, the shirt keeps me fairly warm and works great on cold mornings in the spring or fall when it's about fifty degrees. A lot of times I'll have a tee-shirt on under that.

You'll have to experiment with what works in what temperature for you. Everybody's a little different and everybody has different tolerances for heat and so forth.

You may want to try some of these clothes before you go camping with them. If you buy something, wear it to test out the warmth. Kids need to be watched because it's easy for them to sweat and not think about being totally soaked, and all of a sudden they realize they're cold. Remind them to take a layer off if they start sweating.

FROSTBITE

Frostbite is an enemy if it's cold outside. The temperatures don't have to get that low before your skin can freeze. You need to be educated and prepared. If someone's toes or fingers get cold, you need to know. If it's cold enough there's a potential for frostbite.

Make sure everyone in your party understands the significance of cold digits and frostbite, that way enthusiasm for some activity doesn't result in a nasty injury, especially with kids and older folks.

You may not realize how cold your fingers and toes

are because our extremities often feel chilly during the day. Say you're in a sixty-eight degree room and you go outside for a few minutes, your skin temperature drops to fifty and you don't think anything of that. You just go back inside and heat up. My point is you are used to having these swings in your outer skin temperature, because it just happens. Your extremities chill quicker than everywhere else. If you don't take that seriously, it would be possible for frostbite to creep up on you. You saw the signs in the back of your mind but didn't do anything about it, and now you're in the hospital getting treated for frostbite. Teach everybody the signs and keep reinforcing them. If somebody gets cold, take action immediately to warm up the extremities. Keep in mind that if your head and extremities stay warm, it's a lot easier to keep the rest your body warm, especially in a sleeping bag.

WRAP UP

Make sure to dress in layers. Use wool or fabrics that wick for the layers. Make sure the fabric against your skin wicks and is comfortable. Make sure the outer layer is waterproof as needed. You may not wear your waterproof jacket all the time, but it adds warmth in normal circumstances, especially when it's windy.

ELEVEN

BREAKFAST - DO'S AND DON'TS

The challenge with breakfast is that it's early, and while camping you've got multiple things going on to consider. The first thing is that you're sleepy because you just woke up. Once everyone else is awake, they'll want to brush their teeth, use the restroom, freshen up, and so on.

SOMETIMES THE MOST URGENT NEED IS...CAFFEINE

If at least one person in your party has a caffeine requirement, you need to consider how to meet that. So, for example if you're used to coffee, then consider bringing soda or a cold cappuccino

drink instead. There are options for solving a caffeine craving without ever lighting a fire. So, consider a cold form of caffeine that comes out the cooler, or just sits in the car, depending on the temperature outside. These options allow you to either take your time building a fire or not build one in the morning at all.

THE KELTY POT

A Kelty Pot looks like a big coffee pot but it is hollow in the middle with a stainless steel, steel, or aluminum base. You put twigs in the hollow part, light them, and as the heat rises up the center of this pot, it heats the water in the surrounding jacket. That's probably the easiest way to get hot water. The negative part is that you need to sit right there and keep feeding twigs into the hollow section to keep the tiny fire going. There's really not a lot in that combustion chamber, so the fuel exhausts quickly.

Keep in mind there are places, usually National Forests, where you're not allowed to pick up twigs, branches, leaves, limbs, horn sheddings, therefore you'll need to bring something combustible with you. So check where you are for restrictions. But, if you have a supply of twigs, then that Kelty pot is awesome. They're about a hundred bucks and it's a solid lifetime purchase.

DIFFERENT APPROACHES TO BREAKFAST

Some people don't eat breakfast. Some like a midmorning snack. But, when camping and exerting extra energy, breakfast may be a must. It all depends on who is with you.

One simple hot breakfast option is oatmeal. All you need is some hot water to make it. There may even be sources of hot water if you're at a campground with a short walk or drive.

TO BUILD A FIRE, OR NOT

The next thing you've got to consider is where you are. There are locations where you cannot build a fire for different reasons. There are places where there's no firewood.

If you're planning on building a fire first thing, then I would suggest whoever the fire builder is needs to be up forty-five minutes before everybody else. That way you have time to build a campfire and get all of that going before the other people in your group rise.

And the other question is . . . "can you" is not as important as "should you." Say you're in a rush to get a fire going and it's not cooperating, and everybody's ready to go and they're hungry, that doesn't make for a pleasant memory. It might be quicker to stop at a restaurant on your drive to a hiking spot, or to eat something cold from the cooler.

PERHAPS A SMALL STOVE WILL WORK

You light a stove and a couple minutes later, you're starting to heat up a pan full of water, or a frying pan or what have you. The stove is a really great alternative. There are a lot of options. They run from fifty to a hundred-and-fifty bucks. Basically, the traditional Coleman stove type that sits on top of a table has usually two burners. The Coleman stove is ubiquitous when it comes to camping. They have been around at least seventy years. They come in white gas or propane. I would suggest if you're purchasing one buy the propane, because it's the cheapest to operate. There are also small backpacking stoves that are butane, they are small and you can get a lot of fires out of them. The difference is that with a Coleman stove, you've got two large burners, and you can actually heat up a lot more volume of water than you can with a small backpacking stove. There are now one-burner versions from Asian vendors that run off butane. These are small, don't take up a lot of space, and are very easy to use. The Coleman ones are extremely robust. I've fixed many of them with a pocketknife and a paper towel, which is helpful when you are out in the wild.

Pancakes cooked on the stove

So, a small stove is nice because you sit it on the picnic table or on the ground and light your fire and then a few minutes later you've got water for your coffee. If using a small stove, I would recommend testing it at home before you leave. And making sure you have ample fuel.

COLD BREAKFAST OPTIONS

If fixing a fire first thing in the morning is more work than you want, or if your group has an early activity planned, then consider a cold breakfast. Some successful items that I've tried with my family are bagels with cream cheese or peanut butter and jelly sandwiches. These are awesome ways to get something quick that doesn't require a lot of prep or cleanup. A few other ideas are nuts, energy bars, pop tarts, or trail mix. If you have a cooler, you could have cereal with milk, hardboiled eggs, cottage cheese, or yogurt.

On Pinterest or Google, there are many other creative ideas for simple camping breakfast recipes and ideas. You just need to evaluate them based on the need for heat or a cooler, and if those are readily available to you. Can you do it with just hot water? Can you do it with no heat?

WHAT KINDS OF SKILLET TO USE

If you decide to heat over an open fire or a small stove, I highly recommend a cast iron pan. Aluminum pans are harder to cook with over the fire than cast iron. Aluminum conducts heat quickly and changes temperature quickly. If the flame is an uneven temperature then the aluminum won't cook evenly. So I would suggest a cast iron skillet.

COOKED BREAKFAST OPTIONS

One thing that is spectacular about a campfire is bacon. Most mornings we cook bacon or sausage in a cast iron pan. After cooking the meat, I reserve a little grease and then cook the eggs with that grease. I'm telling you, the fact that you're hungry because you're burning a lot of calories that you normally don't and you're out in the woods with campfire smoke lingering, those bacon and eggs will smell and taste luscious. Bacon and eggs is a simple and extraordinarily satisfying meal at a campsite.

Other cooked ideas for breakfast would be sausage, sausage patties, and link sausage. A lot of times adding a little bit of water to help even out the heat helps the sausages cook better.

One thing I would encourage you not to cook is pancakes. They require nice, even, controllable heat which is difficult on a portable stove or a fire. You may be the pancake master at home but pancakes and campfire can be tough. If you really want to try them, bring a cast-iron griddle to help even out the temperature. Even at that I would encourage you to make small, simple pancakes, not stuffed ones as they will get tough because the heat is so uneven.

NIFTY "BURRITO IN A BAG"

A "burrito in a bag" is made up ahead of time. At home, assemble eggs and ham and onions and pepper or whatever you want. Place it all together in a plastic bag. At the campsite, all you need to do is put the bag in hot water. The hot water cooks the eggs and basically makes an omelet. Then, you can eat the food right out of the bag; maybe even use a plastic spoon if you want. That way you don't have a lot of clean up, because your pan's just boiling water. This is an easy and quick breakfast option. The work is done ahead of time at home.

CLEANING A CAST IRON PAN

Your cast iron pan will be much easier to clean than aluminum or steel. A heads-up, if you haven't cleaned a cast iron pan before, it's a little different. You shouldn't soap it up, because it'll absorb the soap taste. Use hot water and a sponge or stiff brush. If the food remains stuck on, mix up a paste of course kosher salt and water to use as a rub.

GENERAL CLEAN UP HINTS

When we cook bacon, we pour most of the grease into a cup to dispose of later. Don't pour it on the ground as this will invite critters into your kitchen area, which you really don't want.

Cooking over an open fire or small cooktop requires clean up time. So, allot at least an hour or more from the time you light the fire until you are prepared to leave your campsite.

To get the cleanup done quickly, try to make it a joint effort. Also, you want to make your cleanup process sanitary because the last thing you want is food poisoning. Make sure to cook meat first, then the eggs in the grease—which will give you really good tasting eggs.

OTHER BREAKFAST OPTIONS

The other thing to consider is what your plans are for the day. If driving to your activity you will pass by a Bojangles or somewhere to eat breakfast, one option is to stop along the way. This will save time in the morning if there are no early risers in the group or no one interested in cooking. Because, let's be honest, cooking and cleaning up a hearty breakfast is time-consuming. Another option, depending on the location of your campsite, one person could get take-out for the group. I think the trick is to size up what everybody's state of mind and the state of their stomach will be first thing in the morning, then base your breakfast meal plan on that. That way you'll have a lot happier people.

BUILDING A FIRE

I go into how to build a fire in another chapter, but

I will say the key to a fire is in the preparation. Before you get to the site as well as while you are at the site. You need some sort of kindling; you need some small stuff, and as the fire grows you'll progress to bigger pieces. And it definitely takes a little bit of time. The more you do it, the better you'll get.

BABY STEPS

I would not suggest full-blown cooking over a fire on your first camping trip. Instead what I would do is have a stove that you've tested ahead of time. It's quick, it's easy, and it doesn't get in the way of that priceless moment. I think after you've had some experience at building a fire and getting your camp kitchen set up how you want it, then breakfast can be a nice, hearty thing.

OUR NORMAL ROUTINE

My wife, Connie, likes to have a nice warm breakfast, so I get up first thing and build a fire. I'll have hot coffee and water boiling in a big pot by the time she wakes up. Many times I'll actually have the bacon started and the wondrous smell is what entices her out of the tent. But, we usually don't do a lot of heavy activities first thing in the morning. I wake up at the crack of dawn, start coffee and breakfast, and we tend to have leisurely mornings.

When we had young children, they were ready to go when the sun rose. That was a time in our life where spending an hour and a half cooking breakfast was not the best choice. A cold breakfast or a meal at a fast-food restaurant worked best for that phase. On the flip side, when they became teenagers they didn't like to get up before noon. In those days, Connie and I were able to have a leisurely morning and cook a hot meal so that when the kids got up, they could scarf down the leftovers and we could start our day. So my point is that you need to right-size it for what your family needs at the time.

BOTTOM LINE

If in doubt, my suggestion is to go with a cold breakfast, something you can do without heat. Keep it simple, and kind of go from there. The point with all of this advice is to know what your skills and abilities are and operate within that framework. Be aware of your plans for the day and make sure breakfast ties in properly, as your focus is on finding that memorable moment.

TWELVE

CAMPING - LUNCH

Let's talk about lunch, and go through a few options that work in a campsite setting. We'll also discuss ways to prepare the noon-time meal ahead of time and eat on-the-go.

HOW TO FIT IN A HEALTHY LUNCH AMID ACTIVITIES.

You're probably going to be busy doing things during the day. Optionally, if your whole day consists of sitting by the campsite and reading or hanging out, then most likely you'll build a fire at breakfast and keep it going minimally all day, and then cook for lunch. Or perhaps you have someone who loves to prepare food over the fire, and will cook lunch. But if that isn't your situation, read on.

Lunch is usually something that can be put together

quickly. That means it is cold so you don't need to tend a fire or cook. For us, sandwiches are one of our go-to's. A really easy sandwich is peanut butter and jelly—it is quick and requires very little cleanup. Another option is a cold cut sandwich. Pick your favorite refrigerated meat and or cheese, and it can keep in the cooler. Another alternative is to use canned or packaged meats or spreads. They don't require refrigeration until opened. You may need mayonnaise or mustard. One trick with condiments is to get the squeeze bottle so you don't need a knife. Another condiment choice is to use the single serving packets, which don't require refrigeration.

One thing Connie does is slice tomato and onion at the house and package it up, so we have a vegetable option to add to our cold cut sandwiches. If you have access to a cooler, you could bring a Tupperware container of tuna, chicken, or egg salad to make a simple sandwich.

PRE-MADE LUNCHES

You can make lunch at home or pick up premade meals at the grocery store before leaving for camp. Alternatively, you could pick up a lunch in the morning on your way to a hike. Throw them in your cooler and your good to go. We hunt down hole-in-the-wall sandwich shops and grab specialty sandwiches in the morning, then enjoy them at lunchtime. The neat thing about places like this is they also offer pre-made basic box lunches.

LEFTOVERS OR STORE-BOUGHT

Don't forget, leftover pizza is tasty cold. Something like Bojangles fried chicken is superb cold. Think about things your family will like and won't mind cold or at least not heated up. The trick with lunch is speed in preparation. You may sit down for a few minutes to enjoy the meal, but then you're going to be on the go again. So, don't get tied up mid-day with some elaborate event, unless that's your choice.

BUILDING YOUR LUNCH

Think about your main course at lunch, perhaps a sandwich or a piece of leftover chicken. Then you'll want something on the side, maybe chips, pretzels, sweet potato chips, sesame sticks, kale chips. Or perhaps you'll opt for an apple, orange, banana, or kiwi. There's a wide range of options here, from healthy to not so much. One thing to consider is how healthy your family eats, camping might be an appropriate time to add those potato chips on the trail as a treat.

LUNCH IS USUALLY IN THE MIDDLE OF ACTIVITIES, SO EAT ON THE GO

Because lunch is mid-day, it lands smack dab in the middle of whatever activities you're doing. Many times you don't want to interrupt those activities, you want to enjoy them. Those are the days when eating on the go works best.

Perhaps you choose to pack your lunch in the morning at the campsite and put it in your bag. You can either eat as you hike or sit down on a rock or an overlook to enjoy the meal. That's a great way to have a nice, peaceful meal appreciating nature. Savor the view and drink in the outdoors.

STAY HYDRATED

Bring water or sports drink to keep you hydrated. These days there are many alternatives, even sugar-free drinks have electrolytes in them. Also, don't forget to clean up your mess, make sure you leave the campsite and trails in better shape than when you arrived.

PLASTIC AND PAPER WARE

Some people are concerned about filling up landfills. Keep in mind the total amount of plastic consumed in one knife is pretty small. Of course you have the option of washing and reusing any plastic products you use. If you use paper products you can burn them in the campfire so you're not leaving that in the landfill. The plastic ware doesn't need to be washed right away, just rinse it off and leave it for when you do the dinner dishes. As long as they are rinsed off, they won't attract bugs, and then you can thoroughly clean it later with hot water and soap.

SNACKS

There are a lot of healthy snacks available. The grocery store has a wide variety from less healthy, empty calorie-type snacks to nutritious.

BJ's and Costco have boxes of individual servings of trail mix, which are convenient to stick in your backpack for the trail. Optionally you can purchase ingredients and make your own with a variety of nuts (cashews, peanuts, almonds), chocolate (either m-n-m's or chocolate chips, but if it is warm, it will melt), mini-marshmallows, Chex mix, cheerios, raisins, cranberries, or any kind of dried fruit. The nice thing about making your own is that you can choose the nutritional value of each serving. Most store-bought trail mixes have a lot of sugar in them. Keep in mind that just because it is a trail mix doesn't make it health food. In fact, some have as much sugar as a candy bar.

Unless it is cold outside, chocolate is probably not a wise snack as it will melt. Energy bars are an excellent option, just look at the nutritional information on the bar. Trader Joe's or Whole Foods tend to have the healthier options.

THIRTEEN

CAMPING - DINNER

Let's talk about dinner, the crown jewel of the meals while camping. We've already discussed breakfast, and though bacon is amazing it takes time and effort you may not have in the morning. Dinner, however, is usually the occasion where you can take more time.

FIRST NIGHT

Let's take a typical four-day camping trip where you leave after work on, say, a Friday. By the time you arrive at the camp ground it's seven or eight-o-clock. You need to pitch your tent before anyone can climb into bed. That first night is probably not the best time to cook a big dinner. I recommend either keeping it simple by eating some type of cold meal, or something you picked up along the way, or do what Connie and I do—eat out, or pick up food on the way and eat when you arrived at the campsite. When you first start camping, do things as simple as possible to make everyone happy. Your goal is to enjoy this time spent together.

Building a fire on the first night is a possibility, though it depends on your skill set. Don't feel obligated to build a fire. You could just eat and go to bed, depending on how tired you are or what you did during the day. It may be dependent on your arrival time.

STOVE OPTIONS

There's the backpacking stove, which commonly use butane gas. They are small, usually one burner, and provide a limited amount of heat.
Another option is a Coleman stove, those big, green things last forever. I fixed one of them with a pocket knife and a Q-tip once. So, they're bulletproof, they're wonderful. They run off white gas, which you can purchase at Walmart and is inexpensive. Though it is very flammable so handle carefully. Always make sure to keep any open containers of white gas away from source of ignition such as open flames, running cars or even electronics like your phone.

You can also find one or two burner stoves that either run off propane or a butane mix. I recommend two burners even though it takes up more space transporting because you can do two things at once. For example, cook you meat at the same time as the vegetables, or perhaps warm up water while you cook your meal.

The downside to a Coleman stove is you don't get the smoky taste from the fire or charcoal. On the other hand, even though there is no smoky flavor, everything tastes better in the woods!

COOKING OVER A CAMPFIRE

I love cooking over the fire. Though I'll admit, I've manned dinner over an open flame a lot and made my share of mistakes. Three years ago, my wife put a week of effort into making gourmet baked beans with hotdogs marinated in. At the campsite I heated them over the fire for about two hours, stirring them to make sure they didn't stick. They smelled delicious, and each time I tasted them my stomach rumbled for more. As I pulled the pot off, I'll be doggoned if I didn't drop it! The pot fell to the side and we lost half the meal. Though it did make for a funny story the next year.

When cooking over a fire you need a grate to sit your pot or pan on, or perhaps you've built something out of rocks. In my situation I had a grate so I had no excuse. Some campsites will have grates over the fireplace. Generally, that's not the case. You can purchase a grate and bring it with you so you have a flat surface for pots and pans—you can even cook food directly on top of a clean grate.

OR A CHARCOAL GRILL

Many paid campsites will have a charcoal grill. Charcoal is easy and consistent. Once lit, it's pretty much trouble-free. The food tastes good. The key with charcoal is to leave ample time to light the coals and get it hot before cooking. Don't forget to put on a pot of water as soon as you take the food off so you can wash and rinse your dishes and utensils. I usually take the water and split it into a container for washing and one for rinsing.

The down side with charcoal is that you don't have a fire to sit by afterwards. However, at some campsites it may be inconvenient or not possible to have a roaring fire. If you do want a campfire, you need to make sure you have wood. As some campsites and national or state forests don't allow campfires, make sure you can have one where you're going.

PLAN WHEN TO START DINNER

There needs to be thought put into when to start a fire or charcoal burning so you'll be ready to cook dinner, so keep that in the back of your mind as you enjoy your day. Perhaps 4 or 4:30 p.m. you may return to the site and begin building a fire or ignite the stove or start the charcoal burning.

If you're using charcoal, you need to start thirty minutes ahead of time to get the coals to the point of cooking heat. I start with the lighter fluid and soak the briquettes for ten to fifteen minutes, then light them. Also, I have a rapid fire chimney starter that helps light the charcoal quicker. They work great and are inexpensive at places like Walmart or Home Depot. Don't forget that with charcoal, there's going to be a peak time where they stay hot, and then you'll need to add more coals if you want to heat water or cook something else. Charcoal definitely needs management.

A campfire will take about thirty minutes to an hour, depending on temperature, humidity, dryness of wood, and how aggressive you are about adding additional logs. The fire needs to burn long and hot enough so you are getting red-hot coals beneath. Once you have a roaring bed of coals, you're ready to cook. As you go through this process, keep in mind that you're going to have to use branches about your forearm size or maybe smaller, perhaps moving up to biceps size once the coals start rapidly dropping. The way to get frustrated is to throw a foot-wide log or green wood onto it. We'll talk more about building a successful campfire in a later chapter. For a quick fire that gets hot fast, use dense wood like poplar. Leave yourself ample time and have plenty of dry wood on hand.

Campfires aren't always successful, so have a backup plan. If you don't have the skill to master a roaring fire, or if the wood is green, or it rained during the day and the dry wood you brought is now wet, or you planned on finding kindling to start the fire but it's either now dark or there was a rain earlier in the day or something else you didn't expect, a backup plan is essential.

START WATER WARMING FOR CLEANUP

Plan for cleanup before you even begin cooking. Once the fire is going, get your big pot and start warming the water. The pot should be about twelve inches in diameter and about a foot tall. So, the whole time you're cooking you're also warming your water. That way, after you're done eating, then you can immediately wash dishes. You don't have to wait thirty minutes for hot water and during that time everybody loses interest in cleaning up. Another win-win.

DUTCH OVEN COOKING

A Dutch oven is a giant cast-iron pot with a lid. It's a great way to cook a lot of things at the same time, either over charcoal or a camp fire, and there are tons of recipes you can find on-line. I'll say a Dutch oven takes a little bit of practice, not a huge amount, but, you might want to steer clear for your first few camping trips. It's a little different to manage than just throwing bacon or ham in a pan, or hamburgers on a grill. The flip side is the foods  you can make in a Dutch oven are savory and worth the effort!

OUR FAVORITE DINNER FOODS WHILE CAMPING

I recommend anything easy to transport and fairly simple to make.

My wife, Connie, is known for her beanie weenies. Everyone raves about them and they are spectacular! She starts days ahead and lets them marinate in their own juices—hot dogs, onions, beans, brown sugar, and Worcestershire sauce. Over your campfire, start it before everything else because it cooks slowly, about forty-five minutes or until you achieve the consistency you want. Cook the beanie weenies too long and you'll have paste, not beans. Either way, the taste is awesome.

We also have had success with Hobo Meals, where you place cut up steak or a formed hamburger, along with carrots, potatoes, onions, then wrap all the food in a tin foil pouch, use heavy duty foil and consider double wrapping as you'll be flipping the pouch over and over as it cooks. You can add butter or oil and some seasoning depending on your taste. Now, based on how long you want to cook these and how you want your meat to come out, you may need to blanch the potatoes ahead of time, or perhaps cut them into smaller pieces. I have a friend who had Hobo Meals as a child and her mother used canned potatoes, that way everything would cook evenly. Do whatever works for you. When we make them, we store them in Ziploc bags, because anything you put in the cooler may end up underwater, so you want to keep everything as water-resistant as possible. Also, you're not spreading the juices from uncooked meat into everything else in the cooler. So, the hobo meals are easy. You throw them on the fire in a fairly warm spot, and then you wait. Forty-five minutes later, you have dinner. Open those up and you've got this nice mixture.

Anything that needs to be sliced or diced, can be done ahead of time at home. Even cutting a carrot at a campsite is a pain. It's also quicker because you don't have that  prep time. The goal at the campsite is to get the fire going where you're getting ready to cook, and at the same time everybody can watch the flames and enjoy the variety of smells.

We also make Biscuit-on-a-Stick. You'll need precooked sausage, a marshmallow stick, and a croissant or biscuit (think those Pillsbury triangle croissants that haven't been cooked yet). Warm the meat over the fire, then wrap the sausage up with the croissant, put it on the end of the stick, and then cook over the flame. Out in the wild freshly baked bread is quite a treat.

Burgers are good over the fire, don't forget the cheese if you like that. Hot dogs and Italian sausages can be cooked with a stick. Chicken can be good, I recommend preparing and marinating ahead of time. Same thing with beef. Just about any meat you can put on a grill usually works really well over a campfire.

Keep in mind that if you have a grate sitting over the fire, you can toast bread as well as hamburger and hotdog rolls.

SIDE NOTE ABOUT COOK SETS

Connie and I bought a whole cook set from Nesco American Harvest which included pots, pans, a sauce pot, plates, and cups. All the pieces stack into this one pot with a lid, and the lid's actually frying pan so it's a great way to transport stuff.

STAY SANITARY

Another important thing is to set up your camp kitchen area in such a way that's easy for you to wash your hands. Because if someone in your group gets food poisoning, y'all will never go camping again! Being sick out in the woods is rough, I know from personal experience. Before you do anything cooking-wise, wash your hands with soap and water. Using the alcohol-based hand sanitizer is not washing your hands, all it does is clean off the outside layer. Say you have dirt on your hands, the sanitizer is not going to remove that. Soap and water is the way to go.

Every time you handle raw meat, you want to make sure you wash your hands really well. Especially because you may be using colder water, which is less effective. So, wash your hands, wash your hands, and keep washing them. It will protect you and everybody else.

USE PAPER PLATES

Instead of plastic plates that need to be washed, consider paper. You can burn them in the camp fire. I'd avoid foam or disposable plastic because when those burn they put off nasty gases. Whereas paper plates, they burn easily. You can carry the unused ones home without difficulty. But do note that even though paper's biodegradable, don't leave a mess. Whatever you bring in, bring out with you. Leave your campsite in better shape than when you arrived.

You may want to save the earth. I will make the argument that this is a camping trip and may be a good time to make an exception from saving the earth in that you're really not talking about a huge amount of volume of plastic, if you use the plastic forks and knives.

S'MORES

What's a campfire without S'mores? They are the *ultimate* camping dessert. A S'more, just in case you don't know, consists of a chocolate bar and a toasted marshmallow between two halves of a graham cracker. Toast the marshmallow over the fire, hot to the point they're about to fall off the stick, and then you put it on top of the chocolate, and between the graham crackers like a sandwich. Squish them together; the marshmallow melts the chocolate, squishes out the side and you have something really good.

You can either find long sticks for roasting or there are metal marshmallow sticks you can purchase.

CLEANUP

So, when it comes to cleanup, clean up quickly.

ENJOY YOUR TIME AFTER DINNER AROUND THE CAMPFIRE

Bring comfortable chairs for everyone to sit in. These days, awesome camping chairs are available for purchase just about anywhere. A lot of them aren't that expensive. Of course, you can sit on a rock if you want to; that's just fine. Or if you want to be a little more cozy, buy a nice big chair that you can lay back in, prop your feet up, and get comfortable. Sometimes the best conversations occur over the flickering of a campfire. Maybe because everyone is so relaxed and out of their natural element, but just sitting by a roaring fire is amazingly relaxing.

FOURTEEN

CAMPFIRE JOYS

The campfire is, in a lot of ways, one of the crown jewels of your camping experience.

In the evening, you're probably somewhat tired and ready to relax and enjoy everyone's company. The most wonderful thing about camping is just sitting around the campfire. Everybody's relaxed. You get to enjoy your family's company in a way you can't do otherwise because we don't have that *sit on the front porch and relax* kind of mentality anymore. But at the campsite, everybody is out of their element and more available for conversation. You may learn something about some person sitting around the fire that you didn't know before because people relax and open up.

As an added benefit, the smoke from a fire will keep bugs away. It's just one of those primal experiences we all enjoy. Make sure if you can have a campfire that you do!

Even if you have to spend ten dollars to buy wood from somewhere, it's worth it. It really, really is.

ALTERNATIVES TO A CAMPFIRE

You may be somewhere you can't build a fire and that's fine, there are always alternatives. Maybe you can find a bluff to park at, put your chairs out on, and watch the sunset. Perhaps there's a park in a town close by with a view. Or, instead of a campfire, listen to some music.

INVEST IN SOME COMFORTABLE CHAIRS

One basic thing to do is sit around the campfire in a folding chair. The now-common camp-chairs, cloth on metal frame, are a wonderful investment. They're inexpensive; you can use them for other things, like going to hear outdoor music. We use ours a lot, we throw them in the back of the car when we go to somebody's house for a barbecue, or sometimes sit on the back screened-in porch in them. Sometimes a campsite will offer benches, but don't count on it. Scope the amenities out ahead of time, you don't want to end up sitting on the ground. There are a lot of options for inexpensive, lightweight chairs.

THE INFAMOUS S'MORES

Sitting around the campfire and eating S'mores is a must-do. It gives everyone something to do while first settling down. Just in case you've never had them, they are a sandwich of graham crackers with a square of Hershey's chocolate and a toasted marshmallow. Yes, they are a high sugar kind of endeavor.

You need something to cook the marshmallow on. You can buy marshmallow cooking sticks at Dick's or any sporting goods store. Or, you can harvest a stick from a sapling or a small tree. Note that there are places where you can't harvest any vegetative matter, so you need to bring your own cooking stick. The nice thing about the metal marshmallow sticks is you can also use them for hotdogs and biscuits-on-a-stick. Yum.

One method of cooking marshmallows is to put it in the hot spot of the fire, wait for it to catch on fire, blow it out and put it on the S'more. This tends to give you a "rare" marshmallow, which means crispy on the outside, maybe not so melted on the inside. Hey, there are a lot of people who like them that way. So if someone in your family, especially kids who aren't as patient, wants theirs rare, smile and watch them enjoy the S'more. I'm more of the take-it-slow, keep-the-marshmallow-higher, and *slowly* cook it until it goes from round to starting to be in a blob and one part starts to drop down. The toasted marshmallow will slightly melt the chocolate. And then

eat your S'more, they are sooo good.

Now I will say just about anything cooked over the campfire is good. You could probably cut the sole off your shoe, throw it over the campfire for a couple of minutes, and come back and go, Wow, I just need ketchup. But S'mores are awesome. How much to pack ranges, depending on the age of the campers. A teenager may eat many more than a calorie-counting adult. For planning purposes, expect everyone will eat two, which should average things out.

POPCORN

Another time-honored tradition is popcorn. Jiffy Pop makes a pan cooked popcorn that comes in a self-contained disposable aluminum popping pan. The trick is to have a long glove so you can shake it long enough for all the corn to pop. Once done, pull the foil with a fork and serve. Delicious.

MAKE SOME HOT BEVERAGES

Another nice thing around a roaring campfire is a hot drink. Either coffee, or instant hot cocoa with mini-marshmallows, or tea, or a simple water with lemon juice. Especially if it is chilly, holding a hot drink is soothing.

FOR COOL WEATHER, A HOODIE

The other thing you want to do is make sure you have a hoodie, depending on where you are, of course. If you're cold, you won't enjoy the evening as much. If you're in eastern North Carolina in late July or early August, you might not need one because it doesn't get that cold at night. If you're out west or up in the mountains, you want to have a jacket to throw on. Depending on how close you are to the fire, you may need some additional clothing. Of course, you can always adjust the distance you are from the fire to kind of self-regulate your temperature. But I would suggest having a way for people to stay warm.

HAVE A BEER, BUT NOT TOO MANY

You can have a beer and relax, that's fine. But be discreet. You don't want your kids' memories of camping to be their dad drunk and grumpy, or combative. The experience is wonderful without the alcohol. So, don't ruin the adventure by drinking too much. There's always the option to not partake. But if you do, keep it in moderation, especially if you're the type of person who becomes an angry or sleepy drunk. You're just going to miss out, and everybody else is going to miss out. Be cautious with your decisions.

On the other hand, if you're out in the woods and someone gets drunk and walks off, they could die of hypothermia or fall and hit their head. Be careful, drinking in moderation is the way to go.

PRICELESS MOMENTS

You will have funny stories around the campfire, and you want to remember them the next day. This is the time when everybody unwinds. You start telling stories, maybe you're laughing about an adventure from the day. Campfire and stories go together. This is a unique experience; it's hard to get that close bond these days as a family. The time before everyone goes to bed is precious, so enjoy.

BE CONSIDERATE OF NEIGHBORS

If you're in a campground, always be considerate of your neighbors. When you start to see other campfires die down and lanterns being shut off, it's time to quiet your group down. Usually what we'll do is light the fire around five, cook dinner, and then sit around the campfire for the rest of the evening. We've gone to bed at nine p.m., we've gone to be at one in the morning. It really depends on the people there. Some groups will hang out and talk and have a great time; other times, everybody's ready to go to bed rather early. It also depends on how demanding your day was.

BE CAUTIOUS OF WHAT YOU SAY

Keep in mind that when everybody goes to bed, tents make a horrible acoustic barrier. Once everybody's in bed, make sure any additional conversation's appropriate for ears that might be listening. Don't assume they can't hear you, because they can.

MAKE SURE THE FIRE IS COMPLETELY OUT

One of the things you want to do when you're ready to turn in is to make sure the fire is out. That means you can put your hand everywhere there were flames and hold it there comfortably. Water's a good way to accomplish that. Another option is about thirty minutes before you want to go to bed, start spreading out the coals. Fire requires heat, fuel, and oxygen. Take any of those three away, the fire will die. Those coals will burn for a while by themselves, but if you spread them out and deprive them of heat, the burning process slows down and the coals will begin to cool off.

The reason to spread the coals out is two-fold. One is they begin to cool on their own so when you do go to bed you know what coals are still hot so you can pour water on them, that way there are no hidden coals. The second is if you have a huge pile of coals and you pour water on them, the water may not reach all the hot spots. Those spots may not be obvious and all they need after you've gone to bed is a gust of wind to send a spark into the night and ignite a forest fire. You absolutely do not want to do that. Sparks can be deadly and do massive damage to property. So be safe with your fire.

ARE YOU EVEN ALLOWED TO HAVE A CAMPFIRE?

Before you have a fire, find out if you can have a fire at your campsite. This information will be available when you check in, which changes from day to day. Sometimes when things get very dry, there'll be bans on open flames because the risk of forest fires is too high. This is usually on a county by county basis. If you're in a national or state park, call the ranger station; a campsite, call the office. That's why putting the fire out when you go to bed is so important.

TO PEE OR NOT TO PEE, THAT IS THE QUESTION

If you or your child has the temptation to pee in the fire, there's nothing wrong with that. Just keep in mind you might be cooking over that fire in the same spot the next morning. Or consider the person who has the site next will be cooking there. The area will smell, it's not sanitary. So, my suggestion is just don't. It sounds a lot cooler than it really is. Maybe just remind yourself or your child that breakfast will be cooked there in the morning, and perhaps that will change their mind. I bet you're wondering why I would bring this issue up. But, if you're a male teenager, standing by a fire, at some point this probably crossed your mind.

FIRE PITS AT RENTAL HOUSES

Check to see if there is a pit you can use instead of building a fire in a new spot. A lot of vacation homes have fire pits and offer wood, though ask to make sure. You want to build a fire in a location where there has been one previously, that will add zero footprint to your campsite.

NO HORSEPLAY AROUND A CAMPFIRE

And the other thing you want to think about is no horseplay around the fire. It happens every year. Someone somewhere is horsing around the fire and falls in the coals. It's very dangerous and several days in the burn ward will ruin your trip. Also, try to avoid horseplay after dark as people can fall and hurt themselves.

DON'T ALLOW UNDERAGE DRINKING

Some national forests, state and local parks have no alcohol rules. I had an underage family member sitting by a campfire at a lake, and the game warden walked up in the dark unnoticed. After he figured out who was who, he handed my family member a painful ticket.

ENJOY THE CAMPFIRE!

I hope you have as good a time as we've had over the years sitting by the campfire, just chitchatting. Some of the stories are great, some of the things you learn. Things you realize about people you didn't know before. There's a huge smile on my face as I'm remembering all those precious moments around a campfire.

FIFTEEN

WEATHER AND CAMPING

If at all possible, you want to make sure your first camping trip is on a beautiful weekend, say somewhere seventy to eighty-five for a high, and fifty-five to sixty-five for a low.

NOT TOO HOT

If it's really hot during the day, let's say its ninety and humid, you may not enjoy being outside especially if you're not used to the heat. Extreme high temperatures can ruin a camping trip, particularly if it is one of your firsts.

NOT TOO COLD

On the flip side, if it's really cold at night and you're not prepared, you may not like that either. The perfect nighttime camping weather is when a light blanket or a cozy sleeping bag can keep you warm. If it's fifty degrees out, you need a little more to be comfortable.

What you don't want to do is end up in a situation where you're cold and miserable the whole weekend. Chances are you won't go camping again after that experience.

PLAN FOR WEATHER

This can be difficult because you've got to prepare for your trip ahead of time. One thing you can do is look at the advanced forecast, or in the *Old Farmer's Almanac*, or visit the Weather Underground site (wunderground.com). These sources can actually show the historical weather information for the weekend or the week you're choosing. To expect eighty degree days in February is not sensible, though depending on your location perhaps in May you could get those kinds of temperatures. That will give you an idea of roughly when to plan.

HAVE A BACKUP PLAN IN CASE WEATHER INTRUDES

If the weather forecast is horrible, cancel and reschedule. You may have put some preparation into this but the last thing you want is a flop for your first camping trip.

If you can't cancel, then consider a staycation where you stay at home but go hiking locally during the day. Or you could set up the tent in the backyard so you have the option of going inside. Both options allow you to enjoy special times and not lose that momentum. Later, when you talk about this experience, your kids say, *You know, we didn't go camping but we had the most wonderful weekend because we went and did A, B, C.*

Have a backup strategy for when you are actually camping to plan on going home if the weather gets bad. If home is too far away, think about staying in a hotel. Consider your gear in a parking lot. If you have a truck, you can't just leave it in the bed; it'll be gone in the morning.

Don't necessarily be afraid of a simple rain storm. It just depends on what the weathermen are predicting. If the forecast calls for a hundred percent chance of four inches of rain, you probably don't want to go camping. On the other hand, if there's a ten percent chance of rain, then, eh . . . maybe risk it.

PLANNING FOR WEATHER IS A CHALLENGE

Weather is a guessing game. Both you and the weathermen don't know what's going to happen until it does. It's difficult to predict far out what the weather's going to be. Even just two or three days before can be tough. So, like we just discussed, have a backup plan.

I don't know how many times I've watched the forecast and thought, *Oh, man, it's going to rain all weekend.*

And then the day before comes and things look dry. When we arrive at the campsite it is beautiful and doesn't start raining until Sunday afternoon on the way home, I'm grateful I made the call to go!

AVOID EXTREME WEATHER

A lot of times forecasts change so much. Weekends I thought were going to be wet turned out gorgeous. So just use your judgment. Stay away from extreme weather. If you're not used to being out in freezing temperatures and you're out in the cold for a full twenty-four hours, unprepared, then you're going to give someone reason to be unhappy. Avoid doing that by keeping track of the weather conditions.

The other extreme is hot. Warm and sticky weather during the day may make everyone miserable. If you're out in the sun it's even worse. Hot temperatures at night may make it hard to sleep. By the next morning, everybody's grumpy because they weren't able to sleep.

Try to hit the in between temperatures so you can have a successful camping trip. In North Carolina, we have two windows with extremely nice weather, from late May to late June and then again from September to mid-October. Somewhere in there is a good rule of thumb in North Carolina to hit beautiful weekends. Of course, it depends on your elevation. Also keep in mind that for every one thousand feet in elevation the temperature decreases by two to three degrees Fahrenheit.

ALWAYS BE READY FOR RAIN

When it looks like rain, take it seriously. On the other hand, if the forecast doesn't call for rain, be prepared anyway. Make sure you dress for the elements. The number one thing you can do in mild weather is to have a waterproof jacket. If your upper body stays warm, then you're a lot more comfortable and the risk of hypothermia goes way down.

I'm not saying to spend hundreds of dollars on Gortex® jackets for you, your wife, your four-year-old, and your three-year-old. But you do need to figure out how you're going to keep everybody dry. There are some low-cost and medium-cost alternatives. Since camping gear is seasonal, you can probably buy a nice water-proof jacket from a sporting goods store that's been sitting the shelf for maybe a quarter of the original price.

One time I found jackets for everybody in the family but me, I already had one. I spent fifteen dollars each for two-hundred-fifty dollar jackets because they were two years old and they were on clearance at Sierra Trading Post. They weren't super stylish, but in the woods that doesn't matter. I'm a big proponent for not spending a fortune for your first camping trip. Instead, do what you can afford. A lot of people go through the weekend with a plastic trash bag with holes cut in for the arms and head and are just fine.

ALWAYS PROTECT YOURSELF FROM HYPOTHERMIA

Hypothermia is a real risk. Keep appraised of the weather. With modern cell phones and real-time radar, it's hard to be completely surprised by the weather. Keep in mind that you may not have a cell connection.

We've been in the mountains where there is rain on one side of the ridge, but sunny on the other side. Sometimes terrain can have unpredictable effects on the weather so keep that in mind. A quarter mile from your campsite there might be a completely different weather situation.

WATCH OUT FOR LIGHTNING

Lightning can kill you. Lightning can start fires and cause trees to split and fall on your tent. There are a lot of things to consider when you're out camping. If the weather's calling for a thunder storm, or you see one coming in, you must take the lightning seriously. If you are hit, then you can be seriously injured or die. Lightning has the ability to injure multiple people at once, and it all happens swiftly. Make sure to take shelter.

If there is even a chance of thunder when you pitch your tent, consider setting up in the middle of a field instead of under trees. If the wind gets blowing and a thick branch falls or lightning hits a tree, pitching your tent under those trees isn't wise. In the middle of the field may seem counterintuitive but that's probably the safest place to put your tent, that way you're less likely to get hit by falling limbs.

If you are caught in a lightning storm, you need to get out in the middle of a field or optionally low to the ground. Make sure you aren't the tallest thing in that area. If lightning starts in the middle of the night and you're in your tent, stay put. I've ridden out so many thunderstorms by hunkering down. Making a mad dash across a field probably won't help you a whole lot.

We've camped through some nasty thunderstorms. A year ago, we got hit by one with sixty-mile-an-hour winds. The tent was fine, we were unscathed. Some trees fell, but not where we were. We had selected a grassy area for the tent.

We've had a tornado hit while camping. That was an experience! In that case we had to abandon the campsite. I probably had fifteen people in the group. We headed on the other side of the ridge and each grabbed a tree and stayed low to the ground and waited for the tornado to pass over us. Thankfully it broke up a few hundred yards before getting to us, so all was good. But we were prepared. I was pretty confident we'd all be just fine. I also figured we'd be going to the store for more camping gear, but we didn't lose very much because the tornado broke

FAMILY CAMPING

up before reaching the campsite. I'll tell you, it was quite a sight, but we stayed safe by hugging a tree.

TAKE BRUSH FIRE THREATS SERIOUSLY

If you spot brush fires in the area, don't camp there. You need to be in a place where you're safe. If you ever see a brush fire, you want to move at a right angle to the direction its moving. You can't outrun it. If the wind is pushing the fire, it'll outrun you. So, move at a right angle to the direction the fire is moving in. If a brush fire is coming at you, go left or go right and keep going that way to let it pass you. Don't worry if your gear gets burned to a crisp, keep going and stay safe. The best plan is to avoid areas where brush fires are burning.

SOMETIMES WE CAN MAKE MEMORIES FROM IFFY WEATHER

Let me preface this story with the years of experience I have with camping and gear and judging weather patterns. So, as they say on television, don't try this at home. That said, years ago we rode out Hurricane Bob in a tent in the Shenandoah mountains of Virginia. By the time it reached us, Bob was a tropical storm and degrading fast. We didn't know which way the storm would turn but it rained for twenty-four hours. I sat in the tent and played cards with my four and seven-year-old girls and we had a moderately good time. If the weather got real bad, we planned to drive to a hotel. Some of our gear got wet. But we were at a KOA campground with a laundry facility, so we were able to put our sleeping bags in the dryer after the rain ended. We enjoyed ourselves because we were paying close attention to the weather, we were prepared, and the girls trusted me.

Now, if I knew the storm would be a hurricane or a strong tropical storm, we would have left. I paid close attention to what was happening the whole time and didn't feel like we were at risk.

COLD WEATHER

30 degree day on Round Bald, but Connie was ready to go hiking

We've had snow. We've had cold nights. We've had snow on top of our mountain, or at least the next mountain over. Memorial Day weekend we had guests who couldn't leave going in one direction because the snow got too deep on the road. That's not typical in North Carolina in late May, but it can happen. So, having a change of warm clothes is wise, because you might have some crazy conditions at times. Depending on where you are in the U.S., weather can be all over the board. If you're in the high mountains, say 6,000+ feet, you could have snow in July. It just depends on your location. Always expect the unexpected with weather.

Be aware of what the weather typically is in your area and be prepared for that as well as having contingency plans and warm clothes. Those things help keep a trip from becoming uncomfortable or even a tragedy.

Know the forecast, and be prepared for rain. Be ready for cold. Have some options. Because having that sweatshirt and warm pants to throw on for everybody in the family may make the difference between later laughing about, *Hey, it rained - remember that? We got to go out to eat* versus an angry child reminding you they froze on that camping trip and never want to go back. Be ready. Prepare for success and everyone wins.

Being ready for a cold day made this hike possible and comfortable

SIXTEEN

BREAKING CAMP

So you've had a great weekend camping. Perhaps it's Sunday morning and you're looking forward to getting home and taking a nice, long, warm shower, not to mention sleeping in your own bed and cooking at your own stove and sitting in front of your TV in your favorite chair. Except, before those luxuries happen, you need to break camp and drive home.

SAVE TIME ON NEXT TRIP BY BREAKING CAMP IN AN ORGANIZED MANNER

A lot of decisions need to be made when you break down your camp. You may think you're just throwing stuff in the car and heading home. Well, yes and no. This is the time to consider the amount of effort necessary so that you'll have less to do on the backside. Adding a little bit of extra work while breaking down camp can truly help you be in a better position when you arrive home, as well as the next time you go camping.

DON'T PACK DAMP CLOTH SURFACES

Consider several issues. First, ask yourself when the last time dew fell. For y'all that don't spend a lot of time outdoors, dew is small drops of moisture during the night covering cool surfaces. This can be a problem because your tent is now wet, as well as your shelter and any cloth structures you've been using. You don't want to store a wet tent in a bag and forget about it until you go camping again as the moisture will sit on the fabric and create a horrible odor. Mold and mildew will wreck a tent. Also, note that when you leave moisture on a fabric the waterproofing breaks down. So, not only will you have an odor, but you won't want to use the tent and eventually it will leak.

Make sure you examine your tent to check for wetness on the bottom, top, or sides. By wet, I mean damp, *at all*. If it's rained recently, it may be wet. If the morning brought condensation, it may be moist. If your tent isn't completely dry when you take it down, then upon arriving at home, open it up to expose it to the air. Once dry, pack it away. At the campsite, if you're tent is bone dry, then go ahead and roll it up, put it in the bag and you're good to go.

The issue of the moisture can be a bigger problem on

the East Coast than the West Coast. If you're in the high desert, your tent's probably dry so it doesn't matter.

PERISHABLE VS. NON-PERISHABLE FOODS

If you've got perishable foods, they need to be dealt with when you return home. Separate those from canned goods you're in no rush to put away.

Also think about what you're going to save in the cooler. Let's say you have a pound of bacon left over. If you're almost out of ice, you may need to stop to purchase more to keep the bacon chilled. This is the time to take an assessment of what perishable foods you have, and of those, which ones need to remain cold.

For non-perishable foods, which foods do you need to restock before the next trip?

SEGREGATE EQUIPMENT THAT NEEDS ATTENTION

For example, you may not have used your axe or hatchet much, so they don't need sharpening. What about your stove, does it require cleaning? When packing, consider these needs. I have a box for equipment that needs attention and another to go straight into storage.

You don't want to spend three or four evenings cleaning and fixing before your next camping trip. Organize while you pack up.

Let's say your stove needs maintenance, perhaps a seal has going bad. If it lands in storage and you forget about it over the winter, then in the spring when you grab your stove—it won't work. Now you have equipment in need of maintenance; you're at a campsite; you need the stove and it doesn't work. So, I think breaking camp is an excellent time to take stock.

Don't take down your tent until you've swept it

ORGANIZE AS YOU BREAK CAMP

With five extra minutes, you can arrange a container of equipment so you won't need to organize it again. For example, we have a camping box filled with non-food items: an axe, a hatchet, a cutting mat, a lantern, a Kelty pot, and a rope. Now, if we use the cutting mat we need to wash that before we put it up. As long as these items are clean and placed in this box when breaking camp, I'm ready for the next trip! The next time we go camping, I just grab the already-organized-and-prepared-box. This means ten minutes spent on the campsite equals the next time I go camping, I've have this prepackaged box. I pack it the same way each time. And so, I've saved myself a lot of time.

We do the same thing with our kitchen box. I pull out the perishable items so it won't have ants or bugs in it later. All I need to do next time is wipe it down, add my perishable foods, and the kitchen box is good to go.

Arrange your gear neatly before packing the car

BE STEADFAST IN BREAKING DOWN THE CAMPSITE

I know it's tough. You're tired and everybody's ready to go. And you're thinking about getting breakfast or lunch on the way. The last thing you want to do is organize. But at the same time, if you'll go through these items and pack the boxes with these tips in mind, the next trip and packing your car is a whole lot easier. It is tempting to just throw everything in the car and then discover you're out of space because it's not packed well. I always kind of cringe at these extra steps because I'm not the most organized person in the world. When I'm trying to break camp, the temptation to cram everything in the car is alive. But my wife has shown me to stay organized and it makes everything easier.

If you've packed up well, the trip home is easier, because you don't have stuff that's sliding around the car that's loose.

POLICE THE CAMPSITE BEFORE YOU LEAVE

Once packed, police the campsite. Everybody takes an area and looks on the ground, in the trees, on the benches, and so forth. What did you forget? Now, as you're searching, you want to look up, down, and straight ahead; because tent stakes can easily be left behind. Other things, like your cell phone might have fallen out of your pocket and it's lying in some weeds. Or a pot was washed and is leaning against the back of a tree.

Check every square foot of the campsite. Because what you don't want to do is forget something important (even something that's not important). You'd hate to leave a wallet or a phone or a kid's favorite toy.

ALWAYS LEAVE THE CAMPSITE NEAT AND TIDY

You want to make sure you leave the campsite in better condition than when you arrived. I always try to do some sort of miniature improvement project. In some places, there's not really a lot you can do.

Leave the campsite better than when you found it

Other places you can do something to improve the place. Now, I'm not suggesting dig a ditch to modify the site.

What I am suggesting is while you cleaned up your mess, you may notice a pile of trash on the other side of the site someone else left, go ahead and clean that up. Always improve the campsite so the next person has an even better experience.

TAKE CARE OF YOUR GARBAGE

Make sure everything you've packed in, you've packed out. Make sure your garbage is taken care of. Now, depending on where you're camping, you may have to carry your garbage out, or perhaps there is a designated trash area. If you're at a paid campsite, there are trash cans to use. Other places might not have them. On a primitive campsite, you may have to bring the garbage home with you.

So, now, when you're thinking about your trash, let's go through a couple things. If you have to carry trash home, pack it carefully. If you use the "poop on a bucket" scheme, then you want to be really, really, really careful with the human waste in those bags. I recommend putting the bag inside a bucket so there's no way it can spill or leak. Make sure the bucket's sitting upright; stabilize it so there's no way the bucket can fall over or the bag can get punctured. Even if the garbage bag is just trash from banana peels or paper plates or what have you, you want to make sure it is sealed up nice and tight so you can get to a spot to drop it off appropriately. Also, you don't want it stinking on the way home.

MAKE SURE THE CAMPFIRE IS OUT

Anytime you leave the camp site, the campfire needs to be out. One way to make sure the fire is out is to lay your hand on the ground where it was. If you can put your hand everywhere the fire was, then it's out. You'll feel the warmth if there's coals.

Countless times, on public lands, I've seen a fire going and people have left. This can lead to forest fires. It's a dangerous practice and in some places can get you a ticket from the park ranger. If you start a fire that becomes a forest fire, you could receive a large bill or even jail time. Starting a forest fire is sheer negligence.

Also, make sure a mini fire hasn't spread. Maybe, on the far side of one of the rocks, there are some hot coals. Look around and make sure that's well taken care of.

WRAP UP

So, hopefully, this helps to give you a framework for staying organized as you're packing up, and as you're getting ready for the next trip. Organization definitely makes a difference. I've become a believer, despite not being the most organized person. It was a challenge for me. But, if I can pull it off, I'm confident you can, too.

Breaking camp in an organized manner means you

don't forget anything, your car is packed well, and your belongings are divided properly. This allows you to be more relaxed when you arrive home because everything is kind of planned out. You know what you have to do. You know what perishables you have a plan for.

All this organization allows for a more peaceful car ride home, an opportunity to seek out those priceless moments from this most recent camping expedition.

Thank you for buying and reading *Family Camping* (Montie's Guide to Camping, Book One). I truly hope your first camping trip is a success. Hopefully the experience will be a gateway to family fun in the outdoors. Camping can be low cost and an awesome experience. Enjoy the hiking, views, and all the special moments you and your loved ones share.

If you enjoyed this book, please review it on Amazon and Goodreads. You can keep up with what is going on in the outdoor world in North Carolina by visiting:

www.montie.com

I'm working on a second book with even more topics on camping. You can find out more about the book at:

www.montie.com/books

Thanks again for letting me share our outdoor adventures with you! When you're ready to launch into the next level, or simply want further information on camping, consider reading my second book, *Skills for Camping* (Montie's Guide to Camping, Book Two). Here's a quick blurb:

> Written for beginner to semi-seasoned outdoor-enthusiasts, this book delves into how to select gear, effective ways to set up your campsite, safe drinking water, shower options, and more. The word "camping" inspires smiles in many people. Learn how to escape your daily life and create memorable family experiences in the woods.

I knew that would interest you! Check out the hiking chapter from *Skills for Camping* (MONTIE'S GUIDE TO CAMPING, Book Two) below.

HIKING

You either hike to enjoy the journey or to get to your destination. Which are you?

When you're family camping, it really doesn't matter if you get to the end of the trail or not, because that's not necessarily your goal. One purpose is to have an adventure. The adventure could be a micro stroll of a hundred yards, or a hike of three miles. It could be six miles. It *really* depends on who's in the group, their physical fitness, and how interested they are in walking a long distance.

You may find you and your spouse have very different capacities for hiking. And that's just fine. You may find you like to work out and go hiking with your buddies and she goes hiking with you because you enjoy it. Now, if she doesn't work out and she's not used to climbing over rocks and walking over rough terrain, then she will tire quicker than you. I know one couple where the opposite is true. Addressing the comfort and capabilities of everyone in the group is critical to the success of your adventure.

WHAT MAKES A TRAIL DIFFICULT

The difficulty of the mileage depends on the difficulty of the trail. Several factors impact the difficulty rating. One is the trail conditions. If, with every stride, you're stepping over three-foot rocks, it's going to wear you out. Another is gaining or losing altitude. When you change altitude, your body has to work to raise your body up to that height. It's kind of like going up or down stairs. For example, you may gain five hundred feet in a mile. And you think that's not much, but actually that takes energy. If you're going to gain two thousand feet in a mile, that's going to take *a lot* of energy because it's very steep. So, you look on the map or the trail head and see how much altitude you're gaining or losing, and then decide. So, if you're hiking six miles and you're gaining a thousand feet in six miles, that's probably going to be a good workout.

If you walk a half mile out and the same back, on a fairly easy trail (i.e., flat and no rocks to maneuver over) then most adults can knock that out and be pretty comfortable. But there again, if you walk a half mile and you gain four hundred feet of elevation, you're probably going to be breathing hard at spots. The difficulty of a trail is an important consideration because you want everyone to enjoy themselves.

The reason why I'm providing these examples is so you can have a basis for judging the difficulty of a trail. Most trails are graded by difficulty, distance and elevation gain. Those three parameters give you a good idea of the effort involved in hiking the trail.

PREPARATION CAN MAKE A DIFFERENCE

If you don't like to hike much, and you know a trip is a month out, I'd recommend you start walking to build endurance and strength. Consistency in the frequency of your workouts is the way to success. If you're not physically fit and you're not prepared for it, you're just not going to enjoy hiking as much. But if you start putting in twenty minutes a day and walk a mile a day at a brisk pace, you will feel a lot better hiking a month from now. This preparation gets you in better cardiovascular shape and builds muscle strength, which means you're less likely to injure yourself. So, even a small time commitment can make a big impact on your ability to enjoy your trip. If you are the only one to prepare then you are in a better position to lead the hiking and serve the rest of your family along the journey.

PHYSICAL LIMITATIONS

If you or somebody in your family has a physical limitation, you need to plan your trip around that. Park websites are loaded with information to allow you to plan as necessary.

INJURIES HAPPEN WHEN

Injuries happen in three circumstances: when people start to tire, during horseplay, and when the trail is in poor condition. Trails with snow or ice can be dangerous, as can be slick rocks.

Back to horseplay for a moment, you have to strike a balance between actions with a low risk of failure and ones that could really hurt someone. If you fall off a cliff, many times you're dead. So, it should be obvious to not let your kid's horse around near a cliff. On the other hand, if you fall on your butt while on the trail, you may not injure anything but your pride. Keep in mind that an injury two miles into a trail may require a team of people to extract the injured hiker.

THINK ABOUT WHO IS IN YOUR GROUP

If you have sixteen-year-olds in the peak of health and play sports, they're probably going to be waiting on you. That's why it's important which trails you pick. It's probably better to have a trail be a little short and then find another hike to do part of, or spend some time sitting at an overlook watching what's going on rather than beat yourself up on an overly difficult trail, saying "we have to get to the end of this trail" and making everyone miserable. The old adage "leave them wanting for more" is a sound goal when hiking.

Watch out getting on long trails, maybe greater than a mile, if you're not familiar with what your capabilities are. It is easy to say something like "it's just six miles", but sometimes six miles can be a long way. If you know what your abilities are, then you already know how far you can or can't go. If you don't know your capabilities, then keep it simple. If you have kids in tow, keep it even simpler. They're going to remember stopping to play in the creek as much as they're going to remember the trail you hiked. Something to keep in mind.

DIFFERENT KINDS OF TRAILS

There are out-and-back, lariat, and loop trails. Out-and-back basically means you go to the end, you turn around, and you come back on the same trail. A lariat means you go and you keep walking but eventually the trail comes back to itself, and then you reverse direction and go back home. A loop is where the trail makes a loop; it may come back out near where you started, or it may return further away from where you started.

TRAIL MAPS AND REVIEWS

When you are considering a trail, make sure to read the reviews. Keep in mind the signature of the reviewer. For example, if someone loves hiking and their user name is HIKE_TO_LIVE, that will have a different connotation than someone named GRANDMA_FOR_LIFE. I'm not saying there aren't some grandmas out there in really good shape. But you can read between the lines and figure out the capability of the poster. One person's "easy" may be a triathlon's easy, versus someone who's not in good shape easy.

MOVE AT A COMFORTABLE PACE FOR EVERYONE

With individual differences that means you're going to end up setting the pace for one person. That's okay. You set the pace for that one person and then the rest of the time you smile, and you laugh, and you hope everybody else does. That's how priceless moments are made. Whether or not you make it to the end of the trail does not matter. What matters is you return safely, and everyone has a great time.

If you're the one in good shape, you love to hike, and you're gung-ho, I'll caution you to temper your enthusiasm for where you're going and not put everybody else in a difficult situation.

DON'T PUSH ANYONE TOO HARD

If you push someone beyond their ability to perform at whatever level they can, then they may not enjoy this hike. They may not enjoy the rest of the day. Or they may slip and fall and hurt themselves. This is one of those times where kindness and love and joy can abound. And you just have to roll with the punches.

The point is to enjoy the day, no matter how easy the trail may be. Concentrate on your children's laughter and comments, and having a really great time of it all, instead of the ease of the trail.

SHOES FOR HIKING

Appropriate hiking shoes are imperative. This is where you're just going to have to make some decisions. If you're planning to hike miles, then your shoes need to protect your feet from the rigors of the trail.

I've got a pair of Asolo boots I've worn for years. It's my second pair of the same exact boot. When I wear these out I'll buy another. They aren't cheap, but the investment is worth it. Hiking boots and your waterproof jacket are the most important equipment for camping. Don't skimp on your boots if you are going to be hiking long distances. You'll want to take your time and find a pair that fit PERFECTLY. Stores like REI will take the time to make sure you have a perfect fit. Anything less is a fit you will regret on a long trail. Poor fitting boots can lead to nasty blisters. Back up your boots with hiking appropriate socks that wick moisture away from your feet.

Hiking boots will protect your feet from damage by rocks. Imagine you're stepping over uneven ground, if you're wearing tennis shoes they will conform to the rock which means your foot can only conform so far. This will lead to bruising, or worse you can hurt yourself.

Whereas a hiking boot is somewhat stiff, so it provides a stable platform to keep your foot from having to try to bend and flex around obstacles. Trail running shoes are in-between a tennis shoe and a hiking boot. You may scoff but your hard-soled work boots are good for hiking. In a lot of ways, they may be very similar to hiking boots. The point is to wear a comfortable shoe. If you're walking a half mile on a paved trail, then wear your tennis shoes. But in uneven terrain you'll need more stability.

Let's go back to the "But, it's our first camping trip, Montie," I know, you don't have to go to REI and spend hundreds of dollars.

A nice pair of new hiking boots will cost you between one and two hundred dollars. Or you could pick up a pair of barely-used Hi-Tec hiking boots for fifty dollars from Sierra Trading Post. You just have to decide where your budget and needs fall. I emphasize that if you will be car camping and not going on long difficult hikes, then make do with the shoes you have, assuming you won't be hiking over uneven terrain. You can upgrade later.

WHAT DO YOU NEED ON A HIKE?

When you're hiking, you need to have the right clothes. In other chapters we've talked about how to stay warm and dry. When you traverse more than a few hundred yards from the car, you need to have a jacket and some of the things we've previously talked about. This waterproof jacket is good for rain and to keep you warm. Remember, if you stay warm and dry, you stay alive.

Take bottled water so you can stay well hydrated. Take some snacks for energy. Be prepared with what you need to survive the night if someone becomes injured or lost. Getting wet, cold and dying of hypothermia is a real risk in those situations. Many people have died of hypothermia when they got lost without realizing they are less than one hundred yards from safety. If you are on a trail and there is an injury, it may be several hours to a day before help arrives (depending on the location and how long it takes for help to arrive). Always keep these things in mind.

Give everybody a pack, or you carry a pack with everyone's stuff in it. Take a flashlight, just in case. Take a way for everybody to stay dry and warm.

If there's cell service, take your phone. If you don't have a hardcopy map of the trail, you can download it to your phone in case you lose service and get lost. Just keep in mind that paper maps always work, they don't have batteries to die and won't break when they are dropped or get wet.

STOP AND ENJOY THE VIEWS WHEN YOU CAN

Hiking gives you the ability to go a place you wouldn't otherwise go. At points when you're hiking, there are times where the trail and the view are beautiful. I'd encourage you to stop and take in the views, especially in the mountains where you have gorgeous panoramic vistas.

Stop. Sit. Chat. Laugh. Love. Wait for the priceless moment. It's not important to be focused on how many miles you've done, but instead spotlight the many smiles you've had.

You've hiked, you've burned calories, and now you're reaping the benefits in this beautiful, relaxing spot. Clouds go underneath you, or horses roam on the barrier islands of North Carolina, or whatever amazing sight, just take it in. Leave your cares behind, this is your reward.

WHEN YOUR DAY DOESN'T GO ACCORDING TO THE PLAN

If you push everybody too hard the likelihood someone's going to slip and fall goes up. A fall may make everyone in the group not enjoy this hike. They may not enjoy the rest of the day. Or if somebody twists an ankle and you get mad at them, they'll remember the moment of anger. This is one of those times where kindness and love and joy can abound. If your daughter twists her ankle and you have to carry her out, she will never, ever forget your kind actions. Twenty years from now she will recall how she twisted her ankle and her dad carried out. When that happens, twenty years from now that trail's going to be, like, six times as long. "It was seventeen miles my dad carried me out." I'm kidding about that. But, they're not going to minimize what you did for them. The story is going to grow, like a fishing tale.

However, if she breaks her ankle, then her memory may be very different and she may never want to go hiking or camping again. Protect your family and your kids from injury. The trick here is if somebody does twist an ankle, smile, help them, and keep going. Get back to the car, drive to pick up some ice, make an ice pack with a Ziploc baggie. Don't look at it as ruining the day. Look at it as a family story. If someone falls and they get a boo-boo, well it turns into a story with value. These stories are told and retold. Make the day an adventure full of wonderful stories. They're not going to recall if they hiked one mile or four miles or six miles. What they're going to remember is how it felt to go hiking. They're going to recall the adventure. They're going to remember the conversation, the love. Those are the important things. And those are the things you can pull off.

ONLY DO AN EPIC HIKE WITH SOMEONE WHO WANTS TO AS WELL

If you want to do an epic hike, my suggestion is to find like-minded people! You may be lucky enough to have a spouse that wants to do that, but most likely not. Save it for a different time with a group of people who want that crazy-ten-miles-in-a-day-over-rough–terrain epic hike.

EMERGENCIES

One thing to keep in mind, if you are ever in an emergency situation, its critical to remember if you're someplace like the top of a mountain (and this is especially true on tall mountains) your cell may be picked up from someone miles and miles away. So, you need to know where you are—what's the name of the trail, what's the name of the mountain, what's the name of the park—and communicate specifics, including the county and state you are in. That way the 911 operator can locate you quickly.

For example: I'm in North Carolina, in Mitchell County, on the Art Leob trail, because you may be talking to an operator a long way away. Make sure your kids know, and your spouse knows where they are. That way if something does happen and you're incapacitated, say you slip, fall, and hit your head, someone else in your party is aware of the details. Telling someone who's twenty miles away that you're in the middle of the woods on top of a big rock isn't going to get you help.

PLAN THE LENGTH OF YOUR HIKE

Make sure you have plenty of time to return to camp. Know what the weather's going to be and time getting back before dark. You don't want to be on a difficult trail trying to get back in the dark. It's a recipe for disaster. Finish your hiking by about three in the afternoon. On a safety note, that also increases the chance that someone will come along behind you, and if you're injured they'll be able to assist you.

EXAMPLES

There's a trail at Philmont, going up Mt. Rogers, they call the Thigh master. There were a lot of one to two foot, or even higher, steps. The terrain was uneven as were the rocks to climb the mountain, and you have a pack on your back. That was a pretty demanding trail even though it was probably less than a mile up.

Whereas, if you're hiking around Waccamaw Lake in North Carolina, where it's perfectly flat, you might walk a mile and not even notice it. You may just walk and talk and have a good time. And pretty soon, twenty-some minutes later, you've gone your mile. But, you'll find it's usually in between hard and strolling-easy.

When you're in the mountains, normally it's a little more rugged. But there are times when you have trails that aren't. In the same park, some trails are rugged and some aren't. So pay attention to the maps and trail reviews.

A good example of opposites is at Linville Falls where you can take a paved hiking trail up to the top that is wheelchair and stroller accessible. Whereas if you go down and hike around the gorge, that's nowhere near stroller accessible. The lower path is always muddy. You have to step over slippery rocks. It's not a super difficult hike, but it's a lot more challenging than the upper trail that goes to the lookout above the falls. So, in the same area, you can have two very different experiences.

WRAP UP

Family camping usually isn't an epic adventure, but it can be cool. And it can be an adventure. Perhaps it even becomes epic because of the laughter and smiles, not because of the miles walked.

You'll find that hiking is a wonderful way to get around. You see things you wouldn't see otherwise and have a great time. Even if it's a half mile, or six miles, or maybe twelve miles—make the most of it. Enjoy the family time. These will be memories you keep and cherish.

It is way better to have a bunch of mini-adventures throughout the year than have a single epic adventure that may never happen. Enjoy those mini-adventures now.

www.ingramcontent.com/pod-product-compliance
Lightning Source LLC
Chambersburg PA
CBHW052030070526
44584CB00016B/1976